S0-AET-925

MONOGRAPHS OF THE
SOCIETY FOR RESEARCH IN
CHILD DEVELOPMENT

*Serial No. 245, Vol. 60, No. 4, 1995*

# STRATEGIES OF KNOWLEDGE ACQUISITION

*Deanna Kuhn*
*Merce Garcia-Mila*
*Anat Zohar*
*Christopher Andersen*

**WITH COMMENTARY BY**
*Sheldon H. White*
*David Klahr and Sharon M. Carver*

**AND A REPLY BY THE AUTHORS**

MONOGRAPHS OF THE SOCIETY FOR RESEARCH IN CHILD DEVELOPMENT
*Serial No. 245, Vol. 60, No. 4, 1995*

# CONTENTS

# ABSTRACT

KUHN, DEANNA; GARCIA-MILA, MERCE; ZOHAR, ANAT; and ANDERSEN, CHRISTOPHER. Strategies of Knowledge Acquisition. With Commentary by SHELDON H. WHITE and by DAVID KLAHR and SHARON M. CARVER; and a Reply by DEANNA KUHN. *Monographs of the Society for Research in Child Development,* 1995, **60**(4, Serial No. 245).

In this *Monograph,* knowledge acquisition is examined as a process involving the coordination of existing theories with new evidence. Although researchers studying conceptual change have described children's evolving theories within numerous domains, relatively little attention has been given to the mechanisms by means of which theories are formed and revised and knowledge is thereby acquired. Central to the present work is the claim that strategies of knowledge acquisition may vary significantly across (as well as within) individuals and can be conceptualized within a developmental framework.

To study these strategies and their development, we use a microgenetic method. Our application of the method allows extended observation of the acquisition of knowledge within a domain, of the strategies used to acquire this knowledge, and of the change in these strategies over time. The method also allows qualitative analysis of individuals and quantitative analysis of groups to be used in complementary ways.

Knowledge acquisition processes were examined at two age levels. Community college adults and preadolescents participated in two 30–45-min individual sessions each week over a 10-week period. Subjects worked on problems involving a broad range of content from both physical and social domains. A transfer design was situated within this microgenetic framework, for the purpose of assessing generality of strategies with the introduction of new content.

Subjects of both ages showed progress across the 10 weeks in the level of strategies used as well as similarity in the form that this progress took. Despite initial performance levels that did not vary greatly, children showed less strategic improvement than adults and inferior knowledge acquisition. Strategic progress was maintained by both groups when new problem content was introduced midway through the sessions. The results thus indicate significant generality of strategies and strategy change across content, as well as populations. A further indication of generality was the emergence of new strategies at about the same time in the social and physical domains, even though performance in the social domain overall lagged behind that in the physical domain.

At the individual level, mixed usage of valid and invalid strategies was the norm. This finding in an adult population suggests that this variability is a more general characteristic of human performance, rather than one unique to states of developmental transition. Another broad implication of this variability is that single-occasion assessment may provide an at best incomplete, and often misleading, characterization of an individual's approach. Still another implication is that at least part of variability in performance across content resides in the subject, rather than exclusively in the task.

That superior strategies present in an individual's repertory are not always applied highlights the fact that more is involved in competent performance than the ability to execute effective strategies. Metastrategic competence—the ability to reflect on and manage strategic knowledge—and metacognitive competence—the ability to reflect on the content of one's knowledge—are emphasized as critical components of cognitive development. These competencies determine the strategies that are actually used, among those potentially available, and therefore the effectiveness of an individual's performance. Finally, the presence of multiple strategies and multiple forms of competence greatly complicates the portrayal of developmental change. Rather than a unidimensional transition from *a* to *b*, the change process must be conceptualized in terms of multiple components following individual (although not independent) paths.

# I. INTRODUCTION

Knowledge acquisition is a process fundamental to survival that begins early and continues throughout the life span. What do we know of the process? Research within the last decade has made it clear that from an early age knowledge is organized into theories that are elaborated and revised over time and that serve as vehicles for understanding the world. In other words, knowledge acquisition to a large degree occurs through a process of theory formation and revision. Among researchers adopting a knowledge- or theory-based approach to cognitive development, the focus has been on describing the content of these evolving theories in a wide range of domains, and we now know a good deal about the progressively more elaborated knowledge that children of various ages are likely to have within numerous content domains (Gelman & Wellman, in press; Wellman & Gelman, 1992).

In contrast, relatively little attention has been given to the process of knowledge acquisition itself, that is, the mechanisms by means of which theories are formed and revised and knowledge is thereby acquired. It is this topic that is the focus of the present work. Within the knowledge-based approach, the assumption that has been at least implicit, and is occasionally voiced explicitly (Brewer & Samarapungavan, 1991; Carey, 1985a, 1986), is that these mechanisms remain more or less constant across development. The present work rests on a contrasting claim that strategies of knowledge acquisition vary significantly across (as well as within) individuals and can be conceptualized in developmental terms.

## KNOWLEDGE ACQUISITION AS THEORY-EVIDENCE COORDINATION

The general form of knowledge and knowledge acquisition studied here is that of the relation between one category of event and another. Most commonly, such relations are construed causally (Cheng & Nisbett, 1993), with an antecedent category of event interpreted as influencing an outcome category (e.g., ingestion of food and a child's bodily growth). Underpinning this form of knowledge is a more basic one having to do with how events or objects fit together into categories (e.g., foods, nonfoods, and permanent vs. temporary bodily changes). Although the latter is not examined here, both forms of knowledge involve theories as organizing devices (Barrett, Abdi, Murphy, & Gallagher, 1993; Keil, 1991; Medin, 1989; Wisniewski & Medin, 1994).

Children's and adults' theories about causal relations undergo revision as new evidence is encountered. Hence, knowledge acquisition strategies involve the evaluation of evidence and inductive causal inference. Recent theories of inductive causal inference in adults (Cheng & Novick, 1990, 1992) are consistent with earlier accounts (Alloy & Tabachnik, 1984; Holland, Holyoak, Nisbett, & Thagard, 1986) in attributing prominent roles both to prior expectation (or theory) and to evidence of covariation (of the relevant factors) in fostering inferences of causality. It is difficult to explain not only simple concept formation (Keil, 1991) but even basic conditioning phenomena in animals without invoking a construct that involves expectation (Holyoak, Koh, & Nisbett, 1989). A conception of inductive inference as involving a coordination of theory and evidence (Kuhn, 1989) contrasts with earlier approaches to the development of inductive inference strategies—for example, the Piagetian research on formal operations—in which such strategies were regarded as largely domain independent and therefore equally applicable to any content irrespective of prior knowledge or expectation.

In empirical studies of adults' multivariable inductive causal inference, subjects typically are provided with a set of multiple instances in which one or more potential causes does or does not occur and an outcome is present or absent (Cheng & Novick, 1990, 1991; Downing, Sternberg, & Ross, 1985; Schustack & Sternberg, 1981). The subject is asked to evaluate the evidence and draw inferences regarding the causal status of one or more of the factors. Although this approach can reveal much about how varying patterns of evidence affect inference, it does not lend much insight into the *minimum* conditions for an inference of causality, which may be as little as a single co-occurrence (of antecedent and outcome), even in the clear presence of additional covariates (Kuhn & Phelps, 1982). Moreover, in natural settings, even when multiple instances are readily available, there is no reason to believe that individuals will seek out and attend to all of them.

For both these reasons, we were interested in studying situations in which subjects are free to select the evidence on which they base their inferences, a condition that links the present work to research on scientific reasoning (Klahr, Fay, & Dunbar, 1993; Kuhn, Amsel, & O'Loughlin, 1988; Kuhn, Schauble, & Garcia-Mila, 1992), as we discuss further later in this chapter. Yet the cognitive skills examined in this *Monograph* are, we believe, representative of processes of knowledge acquisition and inductive inference more broadly (Kuhn, 1993). We therefore situate the present work in this broader context. Methodologically, this means that we examine knowledge acquisition across a broad range of domains involving both physical and social phenomena, rather than restricting the investigation to traditional scientific domains.

## THE MICROGENETIC METHOD

To study knowledge acquisition strategies and their development, we use a microgenetic method. The virtues of the microgenetic method as a tool for examining change have been elaborated in our own earlier work (Kuhn & Phelps, 1982) and more recently by Siegler and Crowley (1991). The evolution of behaviors that one observes over time in microgenetic study can serve to corroborate cross-sectional differences in performance. Most important, however, the method offers the opportunity for detailed analysis of the process of change. Later in this chapter, we summarize findings from previous research utilizing a microgenetic method.

An important feature of the method is that changes over time are initiated by subjects themselves, in interaction with the problems materials, rather than by the investigator, who provides no instruction or feedback with respect to a subject's approaches to a problem. The rationale is that increased density of exercise of existing strategies may lead to change that, except for occurring comparatively rapidly, otherwise resembles a naturally occurring change process. The researcher is thereby afforded close observation of the process.

In addition, a third potential benefit of the method is its capacity to provide a fuller, more accurate picture of competence than can be attained using a single-occasion method. If a subject's performance improves after a few sessions of engagement, it tells us that this level of performance was within the subject's capabilities and accordingly should be recognized as part of his or her competence, or "zone of proximal development" in Vygotsky's (1978) terms.

In several respects, the method used in the work reported in this *Monograph* is an elaborated form of the microgenetic method, one that has not been used in other microgenetic research. First, we simultaneously track two kinds of change over time within a domain. One is the subject's evolving knowledge within that domain (specifically, knowledge of the causal and noncausal relations among variables that reflect the structure of the domain). The second kind of change is in strategies of knowledge acquisition, which may also evolve as knowledge is being acquired. In other uses of the microgenetic method, typically only one form of change has been observed, for example, in strategies for solving addition problems (Siegler & Jenkins, 1989).

A second respect in which the basic microgenetic method is elaborated is that we observe change within multiple domains in which the subject is engaged at the same time. Doing so allows us to compare both knowledge acquisition and evolving strategy usage across domains (as well as relating the two to one another within domains). We wished to examine a broad range of domains, involving both physical and social content, to establish the generality of the knowledge acquisition processes being examined. The research design thus stipulated that each subject undergo parallel engagement with one problem in the physical content domain and one problem in the social content domain. A number of considerations lead to the prediction of greater challenge (and hence inferior performance) in the social domain. Among these are the possibly more extensive initial knowledge (whether or not it is correct) in the social domain and possibly greater affective investment in this knowledge (Kunda, 1990), either of which would make the task of theory-evidence coordination more difficult.

A third elaboration of the microgenetic method is reflected in a research design that incorporates a traditional transfer design within a microgenetic framework. The purpose, again, is to establish generality of the knowledge acquisition strategies that we examine. The traditional transfer design used to assess generality of a skill across content domains is problematic for a number of reasons that we need not review here. A further problem arises if (as we show here to be the case) a subject at a given point in time does not possess just a single strategy but instead selects strategies from a repertory of multiple strategies. If so, single-occasion assessment within a single content domain may produce an inaccurate and misleading characterization (since the subject could have selected a different strategy on this particular occasion and might do so on another occasion); in this case, accurate single-occasion assessment of generality *across* domains is precluded.

The multiple-task, multiple-occasion assessment employed here allows us to assess generality in a more dynamic way than is afforded by a traditional transfer design. Each subject worked on a problem in the physical domain at one weekly session and a problem in the social domain at a second weekly session, for each of the first 5 weeks of a 10-week period of observation. At the beginning of the sixth week, new problems within each of the domains were substituted, and the sessions continued for the remaining five weeks. The question we ask is whether the substitution of new content affects the strategies that the subject uses. To the extent that the same set of strategies that a subject uses in the final encounters with the initial problem carries over to the new content, some degree of domain generality (of both strategies and strategy change) is indicated.

A final elaboration of the microgenetic method is to replicate the design with multiple age groups, enabling us to compare the knowledge acquisition process across age levels. In addition to providing further evidence regarding the generality of knowledge acquisition processes (across populations in this case, rather than content), this comparison is important in addressing a more specific question. The pattern observed in our own as well as others' microgenetic work has been one of mixed, or variable, strategy usage, as we describe in the next section. In other words, instead of a single, consistent approach, the subject shows variable usage of a variety of more and less competent approaches, even though the problem environment remains constant.

An ambiguity arises, however, owing to the fact that the subjects observed in microgenetic work have been either assumed or assessed to be in a state of transition with respect to the competencies in question. It is possible, therefore, that the variable strategy usage that has been observed is a particular characteristic of a developmental transition state, as dynamic systems theories of development predict (Van der Maas & Molenaar, 1992). It thus becomes important to ask whether the same variability over repeated occasions would be observed among populations at other than a characteristic age of transition. If it is, it suggests that this variability is a more general characteristic of human performance, rather than one unique to states of developmental transition.

To address this fundamental question, we chose preadolescents and community college adults as the two populations on which to base such a comparison. Previous work (Klahr et al., 1993; Kuhn et al., 1988) establishes the preadolescent age level as one at which the strategies in question are just beginning to emerge. However, some young adult populations show initial levels of performance little more advanced than those characteristic of preadolescents (Kuhn et al., 1988), enabling us to compare subjects of these two ages in a microgenetic design. In addition to establishing whether strategy change occurs at periods other than the typical period of developmental transition, the design allows cross-age comparison of the process of knowledge acquisition as well as of the interaction of knowledge acquisition and strategy change. Another set of questions centers on the effects of the exercise provided by the microgenetic method. Despite similar starting points, does one age group show more rapid evolution of strategies than another group, both having been provided comparable exercise? Does such change differ only in degree or also in form? These questions are central to establishing the generality of knowledge acquisition strategies across populations.

A final purpose of this *Monograph* is to present a method of analysis that combines qualitative analysis of individuals with quantitative analysis of groups of individuals. Observers of the field's progress, such as White (1994a, 1994b), have lamented the limited range of methods to which developmental researchers have restricted themselves. Especially in undertaking to study the difficult topic of processes of change, innovative methods are called for. In particular, the study of individual subjects is receiving increasing attention as an important and neglected method. As a research method, however, single-subject analysis most often is treated skeptically, and even dismissed, on the assumption that it is severely limited by its inability to provide evidence of the generality of the phenomena observed. Here, we undertake to illustrate how individual and group, as well as qualitative and quantitative, modes of analysis can be used in conjunction to provide an enriched understanding of developmental phenomena.

In the next section, we discuss previous research in more detail, in order to situate the present research effort in the context of various lines of work to which it connects. The reader wishing to focus exclusively on the present work can proceed directly to the final section of this chapter, which introduces the inference forms that figure prominently in later chapters.

## THE PRESENT STUDY IN THE CONTEXT OF PAST RESEARCH

### *From Learning to Conceptual Change*

It was only a few decades ago that *knowledge acquisition* and *learning* were treated as synonymous terms, both referring to a process of strengthening of associative bonds between stimuli and responses. In developmental psychology, Kendler and Kendler (1975) deserve the major credit for moving the field beyond a conceptualization of the developing child as a "cluster of interrelated responses" (Bijou & Baer, 1961, p. 14) and delving into the black box that represented mental phenomena. Although the Kendlers' modeling of such phenomena in terms of covert stimuli and responses was highly restrictive, they demonstrated convincingly that the learning process cannot be studied without considering the developmental status of the organism.

That insight remains a central one today. What individuals already know and how that knowledge is organized constrains what and how new knowledge will be acquired. The burgeoning area of research that has come to be known as the study of conceptual change documents the development of knowledge in numerous domains, with physics (Vosniadou & Brewer, 1987, 1992) and biology (Carey, 1985b) the domains that have been the object of greatest study. Extensive literature reviews are provided by Gelman and Wellman (in press) and Wellman and Gelman (1992).

The main tenet underlying and connecting these individual lines of research is that cognitive development can be adequately accounted for in terms of developing knowledge within content domains. As a consequence, findings are largely specific to the domain studied. The major insight that extends across domains is the theory-like organization of knowledge. Even the properties that define simple concepts cluster and mutually support one another. Conceptions of such homeostatic causal clusters, and the mechanisms underlying them, are the "glue" that makes features cohere (Keil, 1991). At a less elementary level, evidence exists suggesting that young children's theories have properties such as consistency, coherence, comprehensiveness, and explanatory power (Brewer & Samarapungavan, 1991; Vosniadou & Brewer, 1992).

As noted earlier, relatively little attention has been given to the mechanisms that effect theory change. When and how does new evidence lead to modification of existing theories? Despite theoretical claims that these mechanisms are developmentally invariant (Brewer & Samarapungavan, 1991; Carey, 1985a, 1986), little empirical work has been devoted to investigating them. Some research has been done to support claims that theory change will be more difficult to accomplish if it crosses ontological categories (Chi, 1992), involves radical (vs. weak) restructuring (Carey, 1990), or violates entrenched beliefs (Vosniadou & Brewer, 1992).

But how should the mechanisms of change be conceptualized? Keil (1988, 1989, 1991) has addressed this question with respect to the formation of elementary concepts, contrasting accounts maintaining (*a*) that such concepts arise out of networks of associations observed in the environment, (*b*) that the process is theory guided, or (*c*) that at some point a developmental shift occurs from the first to the second process. Keil (1991) rejects the possibilities of an exclusive associative network process and a developmental shift from such a process to a theory-guided one, asking how coherent theories could arise out of networks of associations. Instead, he proposes, all concepts represent a blend of an associative matrix overlaid with causal beliefs. Humans have evolved adaptations for building knowledge representations about sets of regularities in the world, but these processes are never completely data driven or completely theory driven.

In the present work, we address a similar question regarding the mechanisms of conceptual change but in this case with respect to the second-order concepts of relations (particularly causal relations) between elementary conceptual categories. We adopt a perspective resembling Keil's that the mechanism entails the coordination of new evidence with an existing network of theories. What are the strategies that an individual uses to achieve this coordination, and do they change with age and practice? Addressing this question leads to the topics of inductive causal inference and scientific reasoning. First, however, we examine issues involved in the study of change.

*Learning, Transfer, and the Study of Change*

The process of knowledge acquisition is likely to figure prominently in any comprehensive theory of human cognitive functioning. One prominent example is Sternberg's (1984, 1985) triarchic theory, in which knowledge acquisition mechanisms are one of several core components of the intellect. But how is knowledge acquisition studied empirically? Psychologists studying very simple, short-term learning processes may be able to observe these processes directly in the laboratory. The study of more comprehensive kinds of cognitive change, however, especially those involving change in knowledge acquisition strategies themselves, poses serious methodological challenges. Developmental psychologists have been in the particularly difficult position of seeking to understand developmental change without observing it directly. As has now been widely noted, the cross-sectional and even longitudinal designs that are the staples of developmental psychology may provide suggestive data regarding change, but they do not afford direct observation of the process (Wohlwill, 1973).

The microgenetic method has been advocated as a way out of this impasse. As described by Kuhn and Phelps (1982), the goal of the method is to accelerate the change process by providing a subject with frequent opportunities over a period of weeks or months to engage the particular cognitive strategies that are the object of investigation. This increased density of exercise of existing strategies may lead to change, allowing the researcher close observation of the process.

In the initial work by Kuhn and Phelps (1982), we chose strategies of wide applicability as a basis for exploring the utility of the method—strategies of inductive causal inference that are fundamental to knowledge acquisition and can be identified in both scientific and informal reasoning (Kuhn, 1991, 1993). In weekly sessions, preadolescent subjects were asked to identify causal and noncausal effects as they freely investigated a domain in which multiple variables played potential causal roles in influencing an outcome. Strategies of investigation and inference did improve in a majority of subjects over the period of observation. In a comparison condition (Kuhn & Ho, 1980), subjects each week were presented with a set of antecedent-outcome instances identical to that which the subject's yoked control in the free investigation condition had selected for examination; these subjects also showed some, but less, change.

Subsequent research (Kuhn et al., 1992; Schauble, 1990, in press), including the present study, has followed this same paradigm of microgenetic examination of inductive inference strategies in multivariable contexts. Meanwhile, other developmental researchers, notably Siegler and his colleagues (Siegler & Jenkins, 1989), began to use the microgenetic method, in Siegler's case in the very different domain of elementary addition strategies.

Among other researchers who have used a microgenetic method in various domains are Bidell and Fischer (1994), Granott (1993), Karmiloff-Smith (1984), Lawler (1985), and Metz (1985, 1993). In addition, a line of Genevan work beginning with a study by Karmiloff-Smith and Inhelder (1974) falls under the heading of microgenetic research. In certain respects, modern microgenetic research connects to work in the genetic tradition of Werner (1948), although the latter was limited to observation within a single session.

Enough microgenetic work has accrued by now to make comparison and generalization possible (Siegler & Crowley, 1991). Studies conducted within very different domains show convergence in several important respects. Most important, they provide a clear indication of what the change process is not—simple replacement of a less adequate approach with a more adequate one. Instead, subjects commonly exhibit intraindividual variability in the strategies that they apply to identical problems, with less adequate strategies coexisting in a subject's repertory together with more adequate ones. The initial appearance of a new strategy, then, does not mark its consistent application. Instead, less adequate strategies continue to compete with it, and, indeed, the more formidable challenge appears to be abandoning the old, rather than acquiring the new—a reversal in the way that development is traditionally conceived. Change does occur, but it appears as a gradual shift in the distribution of use of a set of strategies of varying adequacy. The most recent microgenetic work (Granott, 1993; Metz, 1993) offers a number of additional insights regarding the nature of the change process. We return to them in the final chapter in discussing insights from the present work.

As described earlier in this chapter, a main purpose of the present work is to extend the microgenetic method in ways that address several critical questions. One is whether the variability and change observed in microgenetic studies is particular to subjects in a period of developmental transition or is a more general phenomenon. A second is the extent to which such change is general as opposed to domain specific. Domain specificity versus domain generality of cognitive strategies is a topic at the heart of much current debate in the field of cognitive development (Karmiloff-Smith, 1994). In a previous study (Kuhn et al., 1992), we addressed this question by having subjects work simultaneously in two domains, with separate sessions each week devoted to each. This study provided some evidence of generality in that improvements in strategy tended to co-occur in rough synchrony across the two domains. These findings, however, do not provide an answer to the more traditional question of whether the newly developed competencies would transfer to new content to which the subject had not been previously exposed. This question is addressed in the present work.

Studies of transfer have served as the traditional means for assessing generality: Does a newly acquired competency transfer to a new context?

Whether the subjects are preschool children or college adults, in a majority of cases the answer has been no. Such findings have led to critical scrutiny of the transfer construct (Detterman & Sternberg, 1993) as well as increasingly domain-specific conceptions of cognitive development (Karmiloff-Smith, 1992). Why should transfer to new contexts be expected? Two prevailing conceptualizations of transfer offer somewhat different answers.

In the more common conceptualization, transfer is seen as mediated by a symbolic representation of the problem domain (Brown, 1989, 1990; Gentner, 1983, 1989; Holyoak, 1984; Singley & Anderson, 1989). To the extent that there is overlap between the representations of two problem domains (i.e., the extent to which the elements of one map onto the elements of the other), transfer between the two should occur. In a study by Brown and Kane (1988), for example, subjects had to recognize a connection between pulling a boat ashore with a fishing rod and pulling someone out of a hole with a spade.

A somewhat different conception of transfer (Greeno, Smith, & Moore, 1993) emphasizes the activity that the problem solver engages in. To the extent the activity is common to two settings, transfer will occur. In the words of Greeno et al. (1993, p. 146), "The structure that enables transfer is in the interactive activity of the person in the situation. . . . When transfer occurs it is because of general properties and relations of the person's interaction with features of a situation."

It is this latter conception of transfer that fits our paradigm better than the first one (which is sometimes referred to as *analogical transfer*). The strategies that subjects develop are very broadly applicable across a wide range of content, but subjects learn to apply these strategies only within the context of particular, relatively narrow content. Will these strategies generalize to new and diverse kinds of content?

This classic transfer question is complicated by the findings from microgenetic research. As noted earlier, microgenetic data indicate that, at a given point in time, a subject does not possess just a single strategy but instead selects strategies from a repertory that includes multiple strategies of varying adequacy. Given this situation, assessment on a single occasion within a single content domain may produce an inaccurate characterization of the subject's competence (since the subject might have selected a different strategy). As a consequence, studies that assess competence across domains are even more error prone. To overcome these limitations, in the present work we situate the transfer design in a microgenetic context, substituting new content midway through the observation period. Through this technique we hope to answer a critical question about the generality of the change induced in microgenetic studies as well as to assess transfer in a more dynamic way than it has been approached in the past.

### *Metacognition, Formal Operations, and Scientific Reasoning*

Piaget (1950; Inhelder & Piaget, 1958, 1969) offered an explicit account of a developmental progression in strategies of knowledge acquisition. Young children construct rudimentary concepts of the type examined by Keil (1989, 1991) that we referred to earlier. With the advent of concrete operations at the age of 6 or 7, concepts acquire the properties of systematic hierarchical classes. A further major development occurs with the appearance of formal operations at adolescence, when second-order relations between categories begin to be examined—the skill on which the present *Monograph* focuses.

Piaget's theoretical model of formal operations has been criticized (for a review, see Keating, 1980), and in his later work (Piaget & Garcia, 1991) there is evidence that even he came to regard the model as insufficiently concerned with the meaning of the propositions that subjects contemplated. Empirical research relating to formal operations has been largely focused on subjects' ability to conduct scientific investigation of the relations between variables in a multivariable context, and here, in contrast, Inhelder and Piaget's (1958) pioneering work has been substantially replicated (Keating, 1980; Moshman, in press). Both the methods and the conclusions of scientific investigation are likely to be faulty among subjects younger than mid-adolescence; moreover, as research subsequent to Inhelder and Piaget's has shown, even older adolescents and many adults often perform poorly as scientists (Dunbar & Klahr, 1989; Klahr et al., 1993; Kuhn et al., 1988; Schauble & Glaser, 1990).

Although they did not use the term, Inhelder and Piaget (1958) in effect attributed poor performance in scientific reasoning tasks to *metacognitive weakness,* defined as the inability to contemplate one's own thought as an object of cognition or, in their (1958) terms, to engage in second-order operations on operations. To the extent that such an ability is truly lacking, the ramifications no doubt extend well beyond the realm of scientific reasoning (Kuhn, 1992a, 1993). Subsequent to Inhelder and Piaget's (1958) work, metacognition has become a topic of widespread interest (Flavell, 1979, 1993; Flavell, Green, & Flavell, 1995; Flavell & Wellman, 1977; Forrest-Pressley, MacKinnon, & Waller, 1985; Metcalfe & Shimamura, 1994; Moshman, 1979, 1990, 1995; Schneider, 1985), but the term has been variably and often loosely defined, with the majority of investigators employing it in its initial and more restricted sense of knowledge and management of one's cognitive strategies, particularly memory strategies.

In the present work, we make a distinction between metacognitive knowledge and metastrategic knowledge, a distinction that parallels in many respects the lower-order distinction between declarative and procedural knowledge. Metacognitive knowledge involves awareness of and reflection on the content of one's thought, ranging from simple awareness of the content of one's present or immediately prior thought (Flavell et al., 1995) to reflection on a set of propositions that one believes to be true or chooses to take under consideration (Moshman, 1990). Metastrategic knowledge involves awareness and management of the strategies that are applied in the course of thinking and problem solving (Sternberg, 1984). Both metacognitive and metastrategic knowledge entail treating one's own cognition as itself an object of cognition—a form of cognitive "distancing" (Sigel, 1993).

Both metacognitive and metastrategic knowledge, we will claim, figure importantly in the development of the cognitive skills examined in this *Monograph*. If knowledge acquisition is a process of theory revision, as we have claimed, to accomplish the process in a skilled way the individual needs to be aware of and reflect on a theory (metacognitive competence), coordinating it with new evidence by means of strategies that are inferentially sound and applied in a consistent manner (metastrategic competence). In the total absence of such competence, evidence and theory are not represented as distinct entities. In this case, new evidence may lead to modification of a theory (as it does even among very young children), but the process takes place outside the individual's conscious control (Kuhn, 1989).

There is a problem, however, with attributing proficiency in knowledge acquisition or scientific reasoning to the development of metacognitive or metastrategic competencies emerging at adolescence. Competent scientific reasoning entails a number of component skills, and data exist suggesting that at least rudimentary forms of all these skills are in place well before adolescence. In addition to the metacognitive and metastrategic abilities just discussed, included among these skills are the ability to entertain alternative possibilities, to detect and interpret covariation, and to isolate and control variables.

One study (Richardson, 1992) in particular stands out for its strong claim of early competence. Even young children, the author maintains, readily interpret both additive and interactive effects of three or more variables—a claim that stands in striking contradiction to data to be presented in this *Monograph* demonstrating the difficulty that even adults have with such coordinations. The data from Richardson's study, however, cannot be clearly interpreted for a number of methodological reasons, foremost among them being the failure to examine individual patterns of performance and distinguish them from group data.

The remaining studies of early competence make more modest claims that certain abilities traditionally associated with scientific reasoning are present in rudimentary forms in young children. Sodian, Zaitchik, and Carey (1991), for example, undertook a study to show that young children can distinguish between an assertion and evidence that bears on the assertion if the context is simple enough. They posed first- and second-grade subjects a problem in which some children wanted to find out if a mouse in their house was a large or small one, which they did by placing food in a box overnight. Two boxes were available, one with a large opening (able to accommodate a large or a small mouse) and one with a small opening (big enough for only the small mouse to pass through). The subject was asked which of the two boxes the children should put food in. Sodian et al. (1991) report that 11 of 20 first graders and 12 of 14 second graders preferred the determinate solution (i.e., chose the small-opening box), indicating both considerable competence and considerable development in this age range. Sodian et al. (1991) note that their subjects' performance reflects a differentiation of hypothesis and evidence since the hypothesis (large or small mouse) is distinguished from the evidence that will test it (the food disappears or does not). Note, however, that the potential confusion in this case is not between theories and evidence (mice and food) but rather lies in the selection of the form of evidence appropriate to test a theory.

In a subsequent set of more detailed studies, Ruffman, Perner, Olson, and Doherty (1993) report similar evidence in comparably simple contexts even among some 5-year-olds (as well as 6- and 7-year-olds). In fact, everyday observation confirms that implicit forms of theory-evidence coordination occur at even earlier ages—illustrated, for example, by a 2-year-old who calls her parents into her bedroom with the claim that it is a ghost in her closet that is the cause of a soft "whooshing" noise that is keeping her awake. This child understands as well as her parents that opening the closet door will provide the evidence capable of disconfirming this causal hypothesis, even though she lacks any metacognitive awareness of her own belief states as hypotheses to be coordinated with evidence.

The valuable function served by Ruffman et al.'s (1993) study is to make clear the connection that exists between early theory-of-mind competencies (Feldman, 1992; Perner, 1991; Wellman, 1990) and competencies that figure importantly in scientific reasoning. Both have strong metacognitive aspects. The 4-year-old child who comes to recognize that an assertion is not necessarily correct—that the candy can be believed to be in the cupboard and in truth be elsewhere (Perner, 1991)—has achieved an essential milestone in the development of scientific reasoning ability. This child has made at least a primitive differentiation between what a mind theorizes to be true and information from the external world that bears on this theory. False beliefs, by definition, are subject to disconfirmation by evidence.

Although it has sometimes been treated this way in the literature, metacognition, like cognition, is not a zero-one, present-absent phenomenon that emerges in full bloom at a particular point in development. The position taken in this *Monograph* is that the development of metacognitive competence, like that of metastrategic competence, takes place very gradually over many years and involves a process of increasing "explicitation" (Karmiloff-Smith, 1992) of skills present in implicit form. Metacognitive competence develops from its most rudimentary forms (examined by Flavell and Gopnik and their colleagues in studies to be described shortly) to the more highly developed, explicit forms demanded by the activities in which subjects in the present research engage.

Ruffman et al. (1993) illustrate the evolution of early emerging metacognitive capability relevant to scientific reasoning by asking subjects to reason about propositions as belief states (a requirement not present in Sodian et al.'s, 1991, study). They ensure that subjects do so by explicitly characterizing these belief states as false. Many (although not all) of the 5–7-year-olds in their research judged that a story character who observes a set of dolls who usually choose red over green food will conclude that the dolls like red food, even though the subjects themselves have been told that this is not the true state of affairs (the dolls really like green food, the subject is told). In this respect, the child comprehends the relation between a pattern of evidence and a theory (the contrary-to-fact hypothesis held by the story character). Put in different terms, the child can draw appropriate inferences from contrary-to-fact propositions (an ability that Piaget tied to the emergence of formal operations). In a follow-up experiment, Ruffman et al. showed that this comprehension extends to predictive judgments (e.g., that the dolls will choose red food again). In theory-of-mind terms, these children are drawing appropriate inferences regarding others' belief states (or theories, as long as we agree to use this term in its broad sense), even when they have been told that these theories are not correct. (The material is deliberately designed so that the child's own theoretical preferences are likely to be neutral.)

The portrayal of early proficiency in metacognitive competencies important to scientific reasoning that Ruffman et al. (1993) offer needs to be qualified, however, by other research demonstrating that the period between 4 and 8 years of age is one of significant development of the basic metacognitive competencies that serve as underpinnings of more complex forms of reasoning about propositions. A series of studies by Flavell et al. (1995) showed 3–5-year-old children to have considerable difficulty accurately reporting either their own immediately preceding mental activity or that of another individual, in contexts in which that mental activity had been particularly clear and salient. In contrast, 7–8-year-olds were largely (although not entirely) successful in such tasks. Distinctions between (second-order) representations (and consequent verbal reports) of thinking about an object and (first-order) representations of the object itself appeared fragile in the younger children. The older ones, like children of a similar age in Ruffman et al.'s (1993) research, were better able to make inferences that depended on representations of mental states.

In related work, Gopnik and her colleagues (Gopnik & Graf, 1988; Gopnik & Slaughter, 1991) showed that preschoolers have a limited awareness of the source of their beliefs—a metacognitive ability that figures prominently in the work presented in this *Monograph.* Gopnik and Graf (1988) found that, even in very simple situations, 3- and 4-year-olds could not identify where knowledge they had just acquired had come from—for example, whether they had learned the contents of a drawer from seeing them or being told about them. Performance was significantly improved, however, among 5-year-olds. Some of Gopnik and Graf's 3- and 4-year-olds might even have been successful in Sodian et al.'s (1991) task of differentiating and coordinating a theory (about a mouse's size) and evidence (of food eaten or not) bearing on it, but they showed remarkably little differentiation of theory and evidence at the metacognitive level of distinguishing the representation of what they knew (the contents of the drawer) from a representation of the evidence that had provided this knowledge. Once the knowledge was acquired, the two evidently became fused into a single representation that encompassed only the knowledge itself. Supporting this interpretation are other findings showing that preschool children report that they have "always known" knowledge that was just acquired in the experimental situation (Gopnik & Astington, 1988; Taylor, Esbensen, & Bennett, 1994).

Evidence regarding early strategic (as opposed to metastrategic or metacognitive) competence related to scientific reasoning is largely positive. Ruffman et al.'s (1993) study substantiates that one of several simple strategic competencies entailed in scientific reasoning—inferring causality from covariation evidence—poses no great difficulty among young children, as earlier research had shown (Mendelson & Shultz, 1976; Shultz & Mendelson, 1975). Indeed, this ability is evident at the sensorimotor level in human infants (Piaget, 1952) as well as in nonhuman organisms. By the end of the first year of life, infants have begun to make causal inferences based on the juxtaposition of an antecedent and an outcome. As data in the present *Monograph* illustrate, it is the fact that this inference strategy is overlearned that causes problems.

Precursors to the critical control-of-variables strategy most closely associated with scientific reasoning are also evident. Most elementary among these are judgments of comparison, first in terms of an individual (Can I run faster than my brother?), later in terms of groups of individuals (Can the girls in the class run faster than the boys?). Once the concept of a fair comparison emerges (What if the boys wore running shoes and the girls didn't?), it remains only to formalize the comparison into the framework of a controlled test of relations between variables (gender and running speed).

Case (1974) has shown that, although they do not do so spontaneously, children as young as age 8 can readily be taught to carry out controlled comparisons.

Early developing forms of metastrategic competence are also evident. A skill important to scientific reasoning is recognition of the indeterminacy associated with entertaining alternative possibilities. This skill is explored in a line of research beginning with studies by Pieraut–Le Bonniec (1980). During the early childhood years, children develop the ability to discriminate between situations that have determinate solutions and those that do not or, in other words, to know whether they have an answer—a competency having clear metastrategic aspects. (For a review of research, see Acredolo & O'Connor, 1991, or Byrnes & Beilin, 1991.) The study by Sodian et al. (1991) can also be interpreted in these terms.

In the face of evidence of all this early competence, a perplexing problem is to explain the persistent poor performance of children, adolescents, and many adults in full-fledged scientific reasoning tasks, that is, ones in which they are asked to examine a database and draw conclusions (Dunbar & Klahr, 1989; Klahr et al., 1993; Kuhn et al., 1988; Schauble & Glaser, 1990). Addressing this critical question is an important objective of the present *Monograph.* With repeated exercise, we find, knowledge acquisition strategies improve among most subjects, but these strategies remain error prone and inadequate among many adults as well as children. Microgenetic data will, we hope, provide insight into the obstacles that impede success in these fundamental forms of reasoning and knowledge acquisition. We therefore return to this question after the data have been presented.

### *Inductive Causal Inference in Multivariable Contexts*

It is a curiosity that research on scientific reasoning (originating and remaining largely in the developmental literature) has proceeded independently of and remains largely unintegrated with research on multivariable inductive causal inference (centered in the adult cognition literature). The central difference between the two is a simple one. Whereas studies of scientific reasoning typically involve selecting instances to create a database, studies of inductive causal inference involve presenting instances from a database for examination. In both, however, the subject must interpret the evidence and draw conclusions, these conclusions being the end product of the process in both cases. Kuhn and Brannock (1977) argued that the "natural experiment" situation involved in studies of inductive inference elicits forms of reasoning paralleling those identified in earlier studies of isolation of variables within the framework of formal operations and scientific reasoning.

Although there exists a large literature on the development of causal inference (for a review, see Bullock, 1985; Bullock, Gelman, & Baillargeon, 1982; Sedlak & Kurtz, 1981), with the exception of our own developmental studies (Kuhn & Brannock, 1977; Kuhn & Phelps, 1982; Kuhn et al., 1988) theoretical and empirical work on multivariable causal inference has largely been located in the adult cognition literature. Like much of the literature on scientific reasoning development, the developmental literature on causal inference highlights the child's early competence. As noted earlier, from an early age children draw on covariation information, as well as other cues, as a basis for inferences of causality (Mendelson & Shultz, 1976; Shultz & Mendelson, 1975). Equally important, from an early age they have theories of causal mechanism that influence their causal judgments (Shultz, 1982), a finding consonant with the more recent conceptual change literature.

Within the adult literature, theoretical analysis has focused largely on covariation as the most important source of information about causality. Mill's (1843/1973) "joint method of agreement and difference" identifies covariation as the appropriate basis for inferences of causality, and Kelley's (1967) extensively researched attribution model similarly rests on covariation between antecedent and outcome. More recent investigators have followed in this tradition but have sought to identify more precisely the inductive strategies that mediate between a covariational database and an inference of causality. In empirical studies, typically a set of multivariable instances is presented in written form and the subject asked to judge what inferences can be drawn (Briggs, 1991; Cheng & Novick, 1990; Downing et al., 1985; Schustack & Sternberg, 1981).

On the basis of such data, Schustack and Sternberg (1981) developed a linear regression model to assign weights to five types of covariation information. The first four are frequencies of the joint presence of antecedent and outcome, the joint absence of antecedent and outcome, the presence of antecedent and the absence of outcome, and the absence of antecedent and the presence of outcome. A fifth factor is the strength of competing causes. Although adult subjects show consistency, leading to positive regression weights for the first two frequencies and negative weights for the second two, Cheng and Novick (1992) identify several theoretical anomalies in the linear regression model, for example, the role of base-level frequencies of antecedent and outcome in predicting the likelihood of a causal inference, factors that intuitively should not affect the causal status of the antecedent.

An even more critical problem, however, for such models of induction purely from an empirical database is the sheer computational weight of the task. The four frequencies in the Schustack and Sternberg model pertain to a single potential cause and outcome. Once the causal field is opened to a host of causal candidates (as it is in natural settings), the computational burden quickly becomes enormous. Some means of narrowing the causal field to a set of manageable factors is needed. Different approaches have been taken to accomplishing this objective, but they have in common restriction of the set of potential causes to the "set of events considered relevant by the attributor" (Cheng & Novick, 1990, p. 562). In other words, theoretical expectation on the part of the subject, arising from a preexisting knowledge base, is invoked as a factor in the attribution of causality.

Cheng and Novick (1990, 1992) propose that, within this focal set, inferences of causality are based on estimated differences in the probabilities of the effect in the presence versus the absence of the potential cause. Hilton and Slugoski (1986) specify "abnormal conditions"—those absent in a comparison condition—as the ones likely to be attributed as causes. Both models invoke the distinction emphasized by Mackie (1974) and others (Einhorn & Hogarth, 1986) between causes and enabling conditions. In Cheng and Novick's (1992) model, factors yielding substantial differences across instances will be attributed as causes, whereas factors that are constant across instances will be either regarded as enabling conditions, if they are perceived as relevant, or dismissed as causally irrelevant (and hence excluded from the focal set).

Note that the latter distinction rests entirely on the subject's theoretical belief. Covariation within a focal set of instances may well provide the basis for a judgment of causality, but, when this covariation is absent, theoretical belief offers the only basis for judging whether constant factors are causally relevant (as enabling conditions) or noncausal. Studies in the adult causal inference literature have tended to focus only on inferences of causality, treating inferences of noncausality almost as noninferences. They have not addressed the converse of the covariation principle—evidence of noncovariation over a set of instances as a basis for an inference of noncausality—or in general examined how empirical evidence might play a role in inferences of noncausality.

As discussed in the next section, we see noncausal inference as occupying a prominent place in inductive inference, scientific reasoning, and knowledge acquisition, and these inferences are a central object of attention in the present work. We also pay a good deal of attention to another problem that Cheng and Novick (1992) acknowledge is not addressed by their model—inferences of causality based on spurious covariation of a noncausal factor with an outcome. The fact that we examine inductive inference over a period of time as a database of instances accumulates enables us to observe how a subject may gradually overcome the temptation of this invalid inference strategy as well as more generally how the subject coordinates accumulating new evidence with theoretical expectation. Most studies of causal inference have confined subjects to the presentation of a single set of instances on a single occasion (with data analysis typically confined to the group level). In contrast, we ask subjects to seek out the evidence that they believe adequate to support their causal and noncausal inferences, and we follow them individually in their efforts to interpret this evidence and integrate it with existing knowledge. We turn now to an examination of the inference strategies that individuals might employ as they engage in this task.

## STRATEGIES OF INDUCTIVE CAUSAL AND NONCAUSAL INFERENCE

### *Causal Inference (Inclusion)*

On what evidence might someone base the inference that antecedent *a* has a causal influence on outcome *o*? In the framework adopted here, we assume a multivariable context, and we assume that the individual is able to select instances to attend to. The question facing the individual is whether a particular factor *a* makes a difference to the outcome. For simplicity of exposition, we consider the case in which the identified factors—*a, b, c, d,* and *e*—are dichotomous (two-level) variables. (Certain differences arise if the two levels of these variables are treated as presence and absence, but, again for simplicity of exposition, they need not be taken into consideration here, and the two levels of each variable will be designated by the subscripts 1 and 2.)

A further assumption that we make is that selection of instances is at least partially theory motivated. In other words, the individual's prior beliefs about the causal and noncausal status of the identified factors influence the selection of instances to attend to. This selectivity takes a variety of forms that need not be identified in detail at this point; some examples are the tendencies to select instances believed to produce the most positive level of an outcome (a success rather than an explanation orientation) and to fail to investigate factors that are believed noncausal.

A minimal (but, as we shall document, frequent) basis for the inference that an antecedent *a* and an outcome *o* are causally related—an inference to which we refer henceforth as the *inclusion* of *a*—is their co-occurrence within a multivariable context:

$$a_1 b_1 c_1 d_1 e_1 \rightarrow o_1. \tag{1}$$

We refer to such an inference as a *co-occurrence* false inclusion inference (because *a* and *o* merely co-occur on one occasion). Such inferences are based on only a single instance and are of course invalid since the co-occurrence does not establish that *a* played a causal role in producing *o*.

In the case in which an individual selects at least two instances for examination, an informative second instance would be

$$a_2 b_1 c_1 d_1 e_1 \rightarrow o_2. \tag{2a}$$

Such an instance, with the outcome shown, allows the valid inclusion inference that *a* is causally implicated in *o*. This inference, based on two instances, is the product of a *controlled comparison.*

In most natural settings, however, people do not have the luxury of selecting for observation exactly those instances that would be most informative with respect to the inferences they allow (Schustack, 1988). Furthermore, in situations (such as the paradigm employed in the present work) in which individuals do have this opportunity, they often do not select such instances. A more likely second instance, then, might be

$$a_2 b_1 c_2 d_1 e_2 \rightarrow o_2. \tag{2b}$$

The pair of instances (1) and (2b) do not of course allow a valid inclusion inference. Nonetheless, as we shall document, people commonly make what we refer to as a *covariation* false inclusion inference: the covariation of *a* and *o* over two or more instances is taken as evidence for the causal role of *a* in producing *o,* despite the presence of additional covariates.

Despite the fact that natural settings typically present multivariable instances with no opportunity for controlled comparison, people frequently make correct causal inferences on the basis of covariation in ways that facilitate adaptive behavior. How do they do so? A likely answer is that they do so on the basis of a large quantity of instances of the form of (1) and (2b). Over a larger number of such instances, a person can observe consistent covariation of *a* and *o* (i.e., when $a_1$ is present, $o_1$ occurs, and when $a_2$ is present, $o_2$ occurs), despite the uncontrolled variation of the remaining factors. In the more complex (and more common) case in which some or all of the remaining factors (*b, c, d,* and *e*) also affect the outcome, a greater range of outcomes may be observed (e.g., $o_1$, $o_2$, $o_3$, and $o_4$, with $o_1$ the most positive and $o_4$ the least positive). But, over many instances involving uncontrolled variation, it will still be the case that, if *a* has a causal effect on *o,* those instances containing $a_1$ will overall be associated with more positive outcomes than those instances containing $a_2$. The contrast in the outcomes produced by $a_1$ and those produced by $a_2$ may be perceived even when instances become available sequentially and are separated in time, precluding any precise computation of its magnitude.

We refer to such inferences as *generalized* inclusion inferences. Their defining feature is that they are not based on the comparison of any specific instances and instead refer generally to an entire database of (uncontrolled) instances; one variable is the focus of attention, and one of its levels is perceived to be associated with a different outcome or range of outcomes than the other level. In one of the content domains involved in the present research, for example, after observing a number of uncontrolled instances involving both large and small boats, a subject may conclude, "The big boats go faster than the small ones." The variable of boat size is thus inferred to have a causal effect on outcome.

A problem with generalized inclusion inferences is that, even though they often are correct, they may not be. Specifically, they can be incorrect in two ways. First, they may be correct for the available database of instances, but this sample may not be representative of the true population of instances. This possibility is a particularly likely one because of the likelihood that the selection of instances that compose the available database is theory motivated. If an individual wishes to generate the most positive outcome or is motivated to produce theory-consistent evidence, the alleged positive levels of all factors believed to be causal will be carried along with those that may already have been established as causal.

Assume, for example, that a database consisting of (1) and (2b) (shown above) is available, with *a* a true causal variable and *c* believed causal but in fact noncausal, leading the subject to make false inclusion covariation inferences for both *a* and *c*. In selecting further instances, the subject is likely to continue to select instances in which both $a_1$ and $c_1$ are present (a pattern that we in fact observed frequently and illustrate in Chap. VII). This selection pattern will produce a larger database in which both *a* and *c* covary with *o*. It sets the stage for an incorrect generalized inclusion inference, the noncausal factor having attained illusory causal power through its deliberate covariation with a true causal factor. Illusory correlation and the resulting incorrect generalized inclusion inferences are thus particularly likely to arise when individuals select the evidence on which they base their inferences.

A second kind of incorrect generalized inclusion inference may result from incorrect, or biased, representation of the database, again most likely for theory-motivated reasons. In other words, the covariation between variable and outcome is in fact not present in the available database (e.g., large and small boats produce the same distribution of outcomes in this subsample of the total database), and the subject only asserts that such a covariation exists (a pattern that we also observe frequently). In incorrect generalized inclusion inferences, then, bias in the selection and/or the characterization of the database is responsible for faulty inference.

Generalized inclusion inference is thus a potentially powerful but error-prone strategy for inferring causal relations. In natural settings in which controlled comparisons are impossible, it is the only way of processing covariation information to make inferences of causality (although a number of other well-known cues, such as temporal contiguity, may influence causal inference). For this reason, generalized inclusion takes on particular significance. It may be used as an effective tool of knowledge acquisition, but theory-motivated instance selection and interpretation are the obstacles that must be overcome if it is to do so.

### *Noncausal Inference (Exclusion)*

Let us proceed now to the contrasting case of *exclusion* inference—the inference that a factor has no causal effect on an outcome. As noted earlier in this chapter, noncausal inference has received much less attention than causal inference, with noncausal inferences treated in effect as noninferences. Especially in multivariable contexts, however, noncausal inferences are critical, enabling the individual to remove many irrelevant factors from consideration and thereby focus attention on a more manageable number of factors.

The controlled comparison of (1) and (2a), we noted, allows a valid inclusion inference. The same controlled comparison, with the modification of only the second outcome, yields a valid exclusion inference:

$$a_1 b_1 c_1 d_1 e_1 \rightarrow o_1, \tag{1}$$

$$a_2 b_1 c_1 d_1 e_1 \rightarrow o_1. \tag{2c}$$

The variation in $a$ produces a constant outcome, and $a$ can therefore be excluded as a causal factor in producing $o$.

In the absence of control, however, this inference becomes invalid:

$$a_2 b_1 c_2 d_1 e_2 \rightarrow o_1. \tag{2d}$$

Comparison of (1) and (2d) does not allow a valid inference regarding $a$ because the varying factors $c$ and $e$ may exert their own effects on the outcome. These effects could compensate one another, producing a misleading constant outcome and consequent false exclusion inference.

How, then, do exclusion inferences get made in the typical situation in which controlled comparison is not feasible? Generalized exclusion inference, parallel to generalized inclusion inference, is theoretically possible. Over a set of instances, an absence of covariation between $a$ and $o$ is noted; that is, those instances containing $a_1$ are associated overall with no more positive outcomes than those instances containing $a_2$. However, the absence of covariation would be exceedingly hard to compute over a database of any size, in comparison to the much more readily observed presence of covariation. While generalized exclusion is theoretically possible, our work shows that it is very rare, and even in these rare cases it is dubious whether any processing of the evidence is involved; more likely, a subject's reference to a noncovariation pattern (which may or may not in fact be present in the data) is invoked as justification for a theory-motivated assertion of noncausality.

### *Asymmetries between Inclusion and Exclusion*

An implication of the preceding analysis is that certain asymmetries exist between inclusion and exclusion. As we have noted, generalized inclusion is a feasible strategy. In the case of exclusion, in contrast, the primary means available for excluding a factor as a causal candidate are either the valid strategy of controlled comparison or the invalid strategy of belief-based assumption (typically leading to the factor being ignored in the selection and examination of evidence). Because the required conditions for controlled comparison are infrequently available and may be infrequently used even if they are available, the second strategy is a common one.

A further difference between inclusion and exclusion lies in the relative frequency of opportunity for application, at least in the context that uncontrolled observation offers. Uncontrolled comparisons of two instances are more likely to generate differences in outcome than equivalences since multiple effects only infrequently exactly compensate one another to produce an outcome of equivalence. Uncontrolled observations are thus more likely to offer an opportunity for inclusion than for exclusion. Both these differences help explain the greater attention in general that people pay to identifying causal, rather than noncausal, factors.

If one overlooks its weakness in identifying noncausal factors, the generalized inference strategy can work fairly well with respect to inclusion, as we have noted, enabling people to construct representations of the causal factors operating in multivariable settings with at least some degree of accuracy. The challenge is to select and interpret instances in ways that minimize the bias of prior expectations. Because the method is powerful (in the sense of the amount of cognitive work it can do), it may be resistant to extinction even when the more powerful method of controlled comparison becomes available. Correspondingly, because the controlled comparison method is so seldom available, people are unlikely to recognize its value or power and therefore may be disinclined to make use of it even if they have the competence to do so and the situation allows it. Both these possibilities are of direct relevance to the present research.

An examination of the inference forms that have been identified here and their evolution with exercise is a major aspect of the analysis of the data presented in this *Monograph*. Another is examination of the knowledge acquisition that the application of these strategies yields. First, in Chapter II, we provide details of the method.

# II. METHOD

## OVERVIEW AND RATIONALE

Preadolescent and community college subjects participated individually in two 30–45-min problem sessions per week for a total period of 10 weeks. Four problems involving a broad range of content extending across physical and social domains were employed. A subject worked on a problem in the physical domain at one of the weekly sessions and a problem in the social domain at the other weekly session. At the beginning of the sixth week, new problems within each domain were substituted, and the sessions continued for the remaining five weeks.

At the beginning of the first session, the subjects' own theories were elicited, enabling assessment of how these theories influenced investigation and inference strategies. Theories were reassessed briefly at the end of each session and more thoroughly (with supporting explanations, as in the initial assessment) at the end of the final session with each problem. Our preference for the term *theories* (rather than the simpler term *beliefs*) derives from the fact that these ideas were in fact much more than simple representations of a feature's causal or noncausal status. Theory assessment showed that subjects readily accessed or invented a wide range of plausible mechanisms that could account for the effects they claimed. Thus, although the causal structure underlying each of the problems was simple, subjects' ideas about the effects of the features were not. This contrast accorded with our goal of studying mechanisms of knowledge acquisition in contexts in which the causal structure was simple and well defined but the causal content drew on a rich knowledge base.

Because subjects were asked to engage the task repeatedly, it was particularly important that it be situated within a pragmatic context (Hatano, 1994) that would provide the motivation and rationale for continuing to work on the task. We achieved this goal by asking subjects to investigate the causal structure (to find out "what makes a difference" and "what doesn't make a difference") characteristic of a particular problem domain and to use this developing knowledge to predict outcomes. The interviewer asked a range of questions ("What are you going to find out?" "What do you think the outcome will be?" "What have you found out?") but provided no direction or feedback. The purpose of the questions was to encourage subjects to engage in cognitive activity, without trying to influence the specific direction that that activity took. By means of probes used as necessary, it was made clear to the subjects that the task was to identify the causal relations operating in the specific database being examined, not in other realms of their experience or in all realms in general. Thus, the task does not require subjects to renounce their own theories, but only to recognize the implications that the evidence they access has with respect to these theories and to recognize discrepancies if they exist.

## SUBJECTS

### *Adults*

Adult subjects were recruited from classes at a large community college in New York City. Volunteers were told that the experience would provide practice in thinking skills, and they were given the additional incentive of a $50.00 savings bond to be awarded on completion of the 10-week period. Of the 17 subjects included in the analysis, 12 were female and five male. Subjects' racial and ethnic backgrounds included black, white, and Hispanic, but they were predominantly Hispanic. Spanish was the first language of 14 subjects; the first languages of the other three subjects were English, Ibo, and Akal. Interviews were conducted in Spanish by a native speaker in the case of nine subjects and in English in the case of the remaining eight (the choice reflecting the subject's preference). Subjects were enrolled in a variety of academic and vocational programs. Their chronological ages ranged from 22 to 47, with most subjects in their late twenties to early thirties.

Of 19 subjects who made the initial commitment and began the sessions, two dropped out after the fourth week and are not included in the analysis. One subject dropped out following the seventh week, and one other dropped out following the ninth week. These two subjects were included in the analysis of phase 1 (weeks 1–5) but not phase 2 (weeks 6–10). Sample size is thus 17 for phase 1 and 15 for phase 2.

### *Children*

Children were fourth graders in a New York City public school serving a population similar (except in age) to that of the community college. Their racial and ethnic backgrounds included black, white, Hispanic, and Asian, but they were predominantly Hispanic. All interviews were conducted in English, which was the primary language of 13 of the 15 subjects (although Spanish was often used as well in the home). The remaining two subjects were bilingual, with Spanish the main language in one case and Vietnamese in the other. All subjects were accustomed to hearing and speaking English in school and appeared comfortable with the language.

Of the 15 subjects who began the sessions, 14 completed the 10 sessions, and one dropped out following phase 1 (weeks 1–5). Data for this subject are included for phase 1 only. Of the 15, seven were boys and eight girls. Their chronological ages at the beginning of the study ranged from 8-10 to 10-5.

## PROBLEMS

Four problems were included, two in the physical domain and two in the social domain. A subject worked on two problems, one from the physical and one from the social domain, at any one time, one at each of the two weekly problem sessions. At the sixth of the ten weeks and thereafter, the alternate problems in each domain were substituted. All subjects thus encountered all four problems by the end of the study.

The structure of each of the four problems was isomorphic. In each problem, two of five features present have no effect on the outcome. Of the three remaining features, one has a simple causal effect, one an interactive effect (it is causal only at one level of the first causal feature), and one is a three-level feature having a curvilinear effect.

In designing the problems, our goal was to include two features that a subject was likely to believe to be noncausal, with the effect in fact noncausal (and hence the belief confirmed) for one and the effect in fact causal (and the belief hence subject to disconfirmation) for the other. Similarly, we aimed to include at least two features that the subject would believe to be causal, with the effect in fact causal (and hence the belief confirmed) for one and the effect in fact noncausal (and the belief hence subject to disconfirmation) for the other. Complex (curvilinear and interactive) effects provided conditions for partial confirmation and partial disconfirmation of beliefs (depending on the particular features levels the subject examined). Since subjects' beliefs were not entirely predictable, without custom-designing problems for each subject, these goals could only be approximated. In general, as we detail later, it was difficult to find features that subjects initially believed noncausal. However, extensive pilot testing enabled us to identify features for which the relevant conditions were met in a majority of cases, and we report all results as a function of the beliefs that subjects actually held (reported in the next two chapters), rather than the idealized structure depicted here.

In one case (the boat problem), the effects were actual physical properties of the materials and events involved. In the other three, the effects were artificially constructed. In these latter cases, our aim was to depict effects that were plausible, even though, in the case of disconfirmed beliefs, they contrasted with subjects' initial beliefs. Since subjects were likely to believe that most features were causal, our most difficult challenge was to find features that subjects were likely to believe noncausal but for which a plausible causal effect could be identified. We turn now to a description of the four problems.

### *Physical Domain*

#### *Boat Problem*

A set of manipulable features influenced the speed with which model boats were pulled down a towing tank by a weight-and-pulley system. The subject's task was to ascertain the effects that these factors had on the boats' speed. The problem was adapted from one developed by Schauble, Klopfer, and Raghavan (1991). Apparatus included a tank 1.5 m long, 20.5 cm wide, and 15.4 cm deep, filled with water to a standard level 3.8 cm from the top. The tank had an adjustable floor that could be raised or lowered to one of three positions. In the deep position, the water above the floor was 11.5 cm deep; in the medium depth position, the water was 5.1 cm deep; and in the shallow position, it was 2.6 cm deep. Also included were two wooden boats. The large boat was 22.9 cm long, 10.1 cm wide, and weighed 230 g. The small boat was 12.7 cm long, 6.0 cm wide, and weighed 74 g. Both boats were 3.5 cm high. Each boat had a small hole at the rear where a sail could be attached. Four sails made of wood and colored cellophane were available, two large and two small, each in two different colors, red and green. When attached, the large sails stood 11 cm high and the small sails 9 cm high. Finally, a burlap sack with a 23 g weight inside could be inserted in a recessed area on the top of either boat.

When placed in the water at one end of the tank, the boats were able to travel down the length of the tank pulled by a 1 g weight on a string affixed to a hook at the front of each boat. The string threaded through two low-friction pulleys, one just above the water level, the other raised 95 cm above the tank on a wooden dowel. A wooden pole that could be placed across the tank served as a "starting gate" for the boats. The distance between the starting gate and the end of the tank was divided into five zones. Each zone was defined by colored tape affixed to the sides of the tank, and the end of each zone was marked by flags of the corresponding color on either side of the tank. The first zone was blue, the second yellow, the third green, the fourth black, and the fifth red. Speed was defined by the zone that a boat had reached at the end of a 7-sec traveling period. When the interviewer lifted the wooden pole at the starting gate, he or she began to count 7 sec on a stopwatch visible to the subject. At the end of this time, the interviewer stopped the boat by placing the wooden pole in front of it. All boats progressed past the blue zone to reach one of the other four zones, where it remained in place, serving as a visual reminder of the outcome.

The causal structure operating in the boat problem is depicted in Table 1. Two of the variable features, sail color and sail size, have no effect on outcome. Boat size has a simple causal effect, weight has a causal effect in interaction with size (it has an influence only with small boats), and depth is a three-level feature having a partial, curvilinear effect (the deep and medium-deep levels do not differ from one another but yield a faster outcome than the shallow level).

### *Car Problem*

The structure of the car problem was designed to parallel that of the boat problem, with the major difference that the problem is presented on a

TABLE 1

CAUSAL STRUCTURE OF BOAT PROBLEM

A. EFFECTS

| | |
|---|---|
| Size of boat (S or L) .......... | Small size (S) advances boat two zones |
| Weight (w or -) .............. | Presence of weight (+) retards boat one zone, in small boats only |
| Depth of water (D, d, or s) .... | Deep (D) or medium-deep (d) water advances boat one zone |
| Sail color .................... | No effect—red and green sails yield identical outcomes |
| Sail size .................... | No effect—small and large sails yield identical outcomes |

B. SUMMARY OF OUTCOMES

| Blue (0) | Yellow (1) | Green (2) | Black (3) | Red (4) |
|---|---|---|---|---|
| | L-s, Lws | L-D, LwD, L-d, Lwd, Sws | SwD, Swd, S-s | S-d, S-D |

microcomputer. In an adaptation of the version used originally by Schauble (1990), the subject investigated a microworld consisting of a racetrack that extended across the computer screen and race cars, having different features, that could be constructed by pressing appropriate keys. Once a car was constructed, it could be run by pressing the "go" key. The subject's task was to ascertain the effects of the cars' features on the speed with which they traveled along the racetrack. Four outcomes were possible. Within a standard driving period of 7 sec, a car could proceed from the starting position on one side of the screen only to flag 1 (about a quarter of the way across the screen), to intermediately positioned flags 2 or 3, or all the way to flag 4 (on the opposite side of the screen).

The causal structure operating in the car problem parallels that shown in Table 1 for the boat problem. Of the five variable features, two (color and presence/absence of a muffler) have no effect on outcome. Engine size has a simple causal effect, presence/absence of a fin has an effect in interaction with engine size (it has an influence only with large engines), and wheel size is a three-level feature having a partial, curvilinear effect (medium-sized wheels yield a faster outcome than small or large wheels, which do not differ from one another).

### *Social Domain*

#### *School Problem*

The subject was introduced to the school problem with the explanation that the Board of Education in a big city is conducting a study involving schools all over the city, in order to find out what features of schools do and do not make a difference in students' achievement. In this part of the study, subjects were told that they would be examining five features; these were then described verbally and also illustrated. In order to make the problem comparable in concreteness to the problems in the physical domain, subjects were able to physically manipulate the features by means of laminated drawings, approximately 6 cm square and mounted on Styrofoam, with Velcro backing for affixing to a large poster board. One feature, for example, was presence or absence of a teaching assistant, and the subject was able to represent that feature by affixing either the drawing of the teacher with an assistant or the drawing of the teacher without an assistant in the appropriate position on the board.

Following a review of the five features, the subject was presented with a cardboard file cabinet containing 21.8 × 28.2-cm (8½ × 11-inch) sheets, each containing a fictitious student's name and ID number and filed alphabetically. Each sheet also contained information depicting the student's standing with respect to each of the five features and (initially shielded from view) an "overall summary evaluation" of that student's school performance, in terms of one of four possible outcomes, ranging from poor to excellent.

The subject's task was to examine the evidence in the file cabinet in order to ascertain which features make a difference and which do not make a difference to students' performance. The subject selected records for examination sequentially by manipulating the Styrofoam drawings on the poster board to indicate what kind of record he or she wished to examine, and the interviewer, using a master list, assisted the subject in locating an appropriate record, which was then affixed to the poster board for examination. Once the subject had made a prediction as to the outcome, a paper overlay was removed and the outcome displayed. (An exception was one subject who consistently chose records on the basis of outcomes rather than features and therefore could not make outcome predictions.)

The causal structure operating in the school problem parallels that of the physical domain problems. Two features, sex of principal and noise versus quiet in the classroom, do not affect outcome. Presence of a teacher's assistant has a simple causal effect. Teacher's location during recess (playground vs. teacher's lounge) has a causal effect (with lounge associated with better outcome), but only in the absence of a teacher's assistant (the rationale being that the positive effect for the teacher of interaction with other teachers in the lounge is eliminated by the compensating collaboration with a teaching assistant). Class size has a curvilinear effect, with large and medium-sized classes yielding equal outcomes but inferior to those of small classes.

### *TV Problem*

It was explained that a marketing company was conducting a study of the features of children's television programs that make some programs more popular than others. The directors of the study, it was explained, showed different kinds of programs to a large group of children in an after-school program, and they obtained ratings of how well overall the children liked each program.

The TV problem was in other respects identical to the school problem. Features were described verbally and represented by Styrofoam-backed drawings that could be affixed to a large poster board, and records of individual television programs (identified by a random mixed numerical and alphabetical code) were contained in a cardboard file cabinet. The four possible outcomes ranged from poor to excellent. The subject's task was to examine the evidence in the file cabinet, in order to ascertain which features make a difference and which do not make a difference to the popularity of the television programs.

The causal structure operating in the TV problem parallels that of the other problems. Two features, day of the week the program airs (Tuesday or Wednesday) and presence/absence of humor, do not affect outcome. Presence of music has a simple causal effect. Commercials have a causal effect (with presence associated with better outcome), but only in the absence of music (the rationale being that these two sources of added interest to young television viewers compensate one another). Length of program has a curvilinear effect, with a 2-hour and a 1-hour show equal in popularity but less popular than a half-hour show.

## PROCEDURE

### *Initial Theory Assessment*

The initial segment of the first session with each problem was devoted to theory assessment. The problem content and each of the features were introduced, and the subject was then asked to indicate which features would affect the outcome and which would not. The interviewer asked specifically about any features not mentioned by the subject. Subjects were then asked to explain their theories. For each feature, the interviewer asked, "How do you know that ——— makes a/no difference?"

### *Problem Sessions*

The subject was then invited to begin investigating the evidence to find out for sure what makes a difference and what does not, by choosing the first boat (or car, or student record, or television show record) to examine. The subject was given a notebook with his or her name on it and told that it would be available at each session, "in case you want to keep a record of what you find out."

1. *Design.*—The subject then selected (and helped construct or locate in the file cabinet) the desired instance. In the two social problems, the outcome was concealed by a paper overlay.

2. *Intention.*—The subject was asked, "Before we run this boat/run this car/look at this record, tell me what you are going to find out." A further probe, used if the subject's response was vague, was, "Which features are you trying to find out about?"

3. *Prediction.*—The subject was then asked, "What do you think the outcome will be?" A marker was then placed on the boat tank, the computer racetrack, or the poster board display of outcomes to indicate the prediction.

4. *Interpretation.*—The boat or car was then run, or the outcome (in the social problems) revealed, and the subject was asked for an interpretation:

"What do you think about how this one came out?" and, if necessary, "What have you found out?"

5. *Justification.*—For each inference of causality (inclusion) or noncausality (exclusion) that a subject made, the interviewer asked, "How do you know that ——— makes a/no difference?" If the subject's response to this question was entirely theory based (i.e., made no reference to the evidence), the following probe was added: "Does any of the testing you've done with the boats/cars tell you about whether ——— makes a difference?" (In the social problems, this probe took the form, "Does any of the information from the records here in the file cabinet tell you about whether ——— makes a difference?")

6. *Notebook.*—The subject was asked if he or she wanted to put anything in the notebook before continuing.

The subject was then invited to select another boat (or car, or record), and the entire procedure was repeated.

The second through the fifth sessions with each problem were identical, except that theory assessment regarding each of the features occurred at the end (rather than at the beginning) of the session, in the form of a final judgment for that session as to whether a feature did or did not make a difference. In the final theory assessment at the end of the fifth session, subjects were again asked to explain their theories (as in the initial theory assessment). A subject generated between two and six instances of evidence at a session, depending on time and the subject's wishes, but with the mode being five once the procedure became familiar (beginning with the second session).

# III. KNOWLEDGE ACQUISITION IN ADULTS

We begin with the changes in knowledge exhibited by the adult sample. Two main indicators of knowledge acquisition are examined. One is the qualitative indicator of theory change, as reflected in the theories that a subject espouses at different points during the period of engagement with a problem, particularly the difference between initial and final theories for each of the features. These differences provide an index of the knowledge that subjects gained. The second indicator is a quantitative one of the subject's evolving ability to predict outcomes.

## COMPARISON ACROSS PROBLEMS

### *Theories*

We initially present results regarding theories and theory change summed for each of the four problems, irrespective of whether a subject worked on the problem during the first or the second 5-week phase. The examination of results in this form is important for the purpose of assessing the overall equivalence of the two problems in the physical domain to one another and the equivalence of the two problems in the social domain to one another—since the transfer design assumes such equivalence. Equally important, results in this form allow the examination of overall performance for different types of theory/evidence combinations involving the confirmation or disconfirmation of causal and noncausal theories by simple and more complex (interactive and curvilinear) forms of causal evidence.

A summary of subjects' initial and final theories for each of the four problems is contained in Tables 2–5. Although there is some variation as a function of variability in subjects' initial theories, for most subjects the first feature listed in Tables 2–5 involves the confirmation of an initially causal theory. Comparison across the tables shows that, overall, subjects had little

TABLE 2

COMPARISON OF ADULTS' INITIAL AND FINAL THEORIES: CAR PROBLEM

| | Theory | | |
|---|---|---|---|
| Feature | Initial | Final | Correctness |
| Engine size: | | | |
| Large > small | 15 | 17 | Correct |
| Small > large | 0 | 0 | |
| Noncausal | 2 | 0 | |
| Color: | | | |
| Blue > red | 0 | 0 | |
| Red > blue | 0 | 0 | |
| Noncausal | 17 | 17 | Correct |
| Muffler: | | | |
| On > off | 13 | 2 | |
| Off > on | 0 | 1 | |
| Noncausal | 4 | 14 | Correct |
| Fin: | | | |
| On > off | 7 | 0 | |
| Off > on | 1 | 13 | Partially correct |
| Noncausal | 8 | 3 | |
| Interaction (engine) | 0 | 0 | Correct |
| Don't know | 1 | 1 | |
| Wheel size: | | | |
| Small > med > large | 2 | 0 | |
| Small = med > large | 1 | 0 | |
| Large > med > small | 6 | 0 | |
| Med > large > small | 3 | 2 | Partially correct |
| Med > small > large | 3 | 6 | Partially correct |
| Med > small = large | 0 | 9 | Correct |
| Noncausal | 1 | 0 | |
| Don't know | 1 | 0 | |

NOTE.—$N$ = 17. Entries refer to number of subjects reporting each type of theory at initial and final theory assessments.

difficulty confirming their initially correct causal theories and that there is little difference across problems in this respect.

The second feature listed in Tables 2–5 most often involves the confirmation of an initially noncausal theory. Again, comparison across tables shows that subjects overall had little difficulty confirming initially correct noncausal theories and that there is little difference across problems in this respect.

The third feature listed in Tables 2–5 most often involves disconfirmation of an initial causal theory. Comparison across the tables shows that performance is comparable across the two problems within both the physical and the social domains. Performance does differ across domains, however, with the majority of subjects largely successful in disconfirming an initial causal theory in the physical domain but unsuccessful in disconfirming an initial causal theory in the social domain.

TABLE 3

COMPARISONS OF ADULTS' INITIAL AND FINAL THEORIES: BOAT PROBLEM

| Feature | Theory | | |
|---|---|---|---|
| | Initial | Final | Correctness |
| Boat size: | | | |
| Small > large | 13 | 14 | Correct |
| Large > small | 0 | 0 | |
| Noncausal | 2 | 1 | |
| Sail color: | | | |
| Green > red | 0 | 0 | |
| Red > green | 0 | 0 | |
| Noncausal | 15 | 15 | Correct |
| Sail size: | | | |
| Large > small | 9 | 0 | |
| Small > large | 2 | 1 | |
| Noncausal | 3 | 13 | Correct |
| Interaction (boat size) | 1 | 1 | |
| Weight: | | | |
| On > off | 1 | 0 | |
| Off > on | 13 | 5 | Partially correct |
| Noncausal | 1 | 1 | |
| Interaction (boat size) | 0 | 9 | Correct |
| Depth: | | | |
| Deep > med > shallow | 10 | 8 | Partially correct |
| Deep = med > shallow | 0 | 4 | Correct |
| Noncausal | 5 | 3 | |

NOTE.—*N* = 15. Two subjects completed only four sessions with the boat problem and are excluded.

Examination of the fourth and fifth features listed in Tables 2–5 reveals that initial theories are variable across subjects and therefore that neither the fourth nor the fifth feature involves primarily the disconfirmation of an initial noncausal theory. As noted in Chapter II, pilot testing indicated that subjects tended to theorize causal effects wherever possible, and it was very difficult to find features for which subjects' theories were noncausal but for which a causal relation was plausible. Those instances in which disconfirmation of an initial noncausal theory was called for, however, suggest that subjects did not find it difficult to do so. The most frequent was in the car problem, where eight subjects initially believed the fin noncausal, two the engine size noncausal, and one the wheel size noncausal. Of these 11 subjects, nine (82%) were successful in recognizing the causal effect. The comparable percentage in the boat problem was 63% (five of eight subjects). In the social domain, initial noncausal theories were even scarcer, but success rates were comparable—67% (two of three subjects) in the TV problem and 100% (three of three subjects) in the school problem.

The most salient characteristic of the fourth feature listed in Tables 2–5 is the fact that it involves an interaction effect. Comparison across the

TABLE 4

Comparison of Adults' Initial and Final Theories: School Problem

| Feature | Theory Initial | Theory Final | Theory Correctness |
|---|---|---|---|
| Teacher's assistant (TA): | | | |
| With TA > without TA | 12 | 15 | Correct |
| Without TA > with TA | 1 | 0 | |
| Noncausal | 2 | 0 | |
| Sex of principal: | | | |
| Female > male | 0 | 0 | |
| Male > female | 3 | 1 | |
| Noncausal | 12 | 14 | Correct |
| Noise in classroom: | | | |
| Quiet > noisy | 15 | 6 | |
| Noisy > quiet | 0 | 0 | |
| Noncausal | 0 | 5 | Correct |
| Interaction (class size) | 0 | 3 | |
| Interaction (teacher's assistant) | 0 | 1 | |
| Teachers' activity during recess: | | | |
| Playground > lounge | 13 | 2 | |
| Lounge > playground | 2 | 2 | Partially correct |
| Noncausal | 0 | 10 | |
| Interaction (teacher's assistant) | 0 | 1 | Correct |
| Class size: | | | |
| Med > small > large | 3 | 0 | |
| Med > small = large | 2 | 1 | |
| Small = med > large | 0 | 1 | |
| Small > med > large | 9 | 7 | Partially correct |
| Small > med = large | 0 | 6 | Correct |
| Noncausal | 1 | 0 | |

Note.—$N = 15$. Two subjects completed only four sessions with the school problem and are excluded.

tables shows that subjects rarely reach a correct conclusion regarding the interaction effect, except in the boat problem, where 60% (nine of 15) do so. A possibly influential factor in accounting for this difference is the nature of subjects' theories. Only in the boat problem could subjects readily envision a causal mechanism that would allow the weight to have an effect on the speed of small boats and yet not appreciably affect the speed of large boats. It should also be noted that in the boat problem most subjects' initial theories were in the same direction as the actual effect (e.g., absence of weight is associated with the better outcome).

This condition alone, however, does not ensure success—for the interactive feature in the TV problem, a majority of subjects held initial theories in the same direction as the actual effect, but only one subject discovered the interaction effect. Subjects' explanations of their theories (at initial and final sessions) support the conclusion that a compatible theoretical explana-

TABLE 5

COMPARISON OF ADULTS' INITIAL AND FINAL THEORIES: TV PROBLEM

| Feature | Theory: Initial | Final | Correctness |
|---|---|---|---|
| Music (M): | | | |
| With M > without M | 17 | 17 | Correct |
| Without M > with M | 0 | 0 | |
| Noncausal | 0 | 0 | |
| Day: | | | |
| Wed > Tu | 1 | 1 | |
| Tu > Wed | 0 | 0 | |
| Noncausal | 16 | 16 | Correct |
| Humor: | | | |
| Funny > serious | 16 | 10 | |
| Serious > funny | 0 | 0 | |
| Noncausal | 0 | 4 | Correct |
| Interaction (music) | 1 | 2 | |
| Interaction (length) | 0 | 1 | |
| Commercials (C): | | | |
| With C > without C | 8 | 9 | Partially correct |
| Without C > with C | 6 | 2 | |
| Noncausal | 3 | 3 | |
| Interaction (music) | 0 | 1 | Correct |
| Interaction (length) | 0 | 2 | |
| Length (hours [h]): | | | |
| 2h > 1h > ½h | 2 | 0 | |
| 1h > 2h > ½h | 2 | 1 | |
| 1h > ½h > 2h | 4 | 0 | |
| ½h > 1h > 2h | 9 | 9 | Partially correct |
| ½h > 1h = 2h | 0 | 5 | Correct |
| Noncausal | 0 | 1 | |
| Interaction (humor) | 0 | 1 | |

NOTE.—$N$ = 17.

tion is needed for recognition of an interaction effect. In all cases in which incorrect interactive theories were expressed, the subject offered a plausible theoretical explanation for the presence of such an interaction. (As reflected in Tables 2–5, these incorrect interaction theories were more frequent in the social than in the physical domain, a difference to which we return.)

The final feature listed in Tables 2–5 involves curvilinear effects, which subjects infrequently conceived of in their initial theories. Here subjects also have difficulty, in this case in recognizing and integrating both causal and noncausal evidence (depending on which variable levels are being compared), and the percentage who achieve a correct final conclusion varies from 27% (boat problem) to 53% (car problem), with intermediate percentages (40% and 29%) for the school and TV problems, respectively. Subjects listed as "partially correct" in Tables 2–5 are those who correctly indicate two of the three relations (of equality or inequality) among the three levels of the feature.

In summary, qualitative analysis of final theories indicates that problems within the physical and social domains are equivalent to one another with respect to the discovery of simple causal and noncausal effects. A difference occurs across domains, however, with subjects finding it more difficult to disconfirm causal theories in the social than in the physical domain. With respect to the more complex (interactive and curvilinear) effects, problems within the social domain are equivalent to one another, and problems across domains are, overall, equivalent to one another. Within the physical domain, however, differences occur that are particular to the effect. Specifically, the interactive effect was more readily discovered in the boat problem and the curvilinear effect in the car problem.

### *Prediction Error*

A quantitative indicator of the knowledge that subjects acquired is their error rates in predicting outcomes. Since the problem sessions represented arbitrary stopping and starting points, rather than examining progress by session a subject's performance within each problem was divided into initial, middle, and final segments (each containing a roughly equal number of instances), for the purpose of examining change over time. To compare prediction achievement across the four problems, subjects' prediction error rates for the final (third) segment were compared across problems. (For this purpose data are combined for phase 1 and phase 2, as in the analysis of theories just reported.) Because each problem involves four possible outcomes, prediction error scores ranged from 0 to 3.

Mean error rate for the final segment was .42 (SD = .21) in the car problem and .33 (SD = .19) in the boat problem. In the social domain, error rate was .57 (SD = .28) in the school problem and .36 (SD = .17) in the TV problem. A series of a priori contrasts showed no difference between the two physical problems and the two social problems and no difference between the car and the boat problems. The difference between the school and the TV problems, however, was significant ($F[1, 13] = 10.96$, $p < .01$). Thus, subjects were less accurate in predicting outcomes in the school problem than they were in the TV problem, despite the fact that their final theories reflected equivalent understanding of the causal effects operating in these two problems. Furthermore, the difference noted earlier favoring the physical over the social domain with respect to correctness of final theories was not reflected in a lower prediction error rate in the physical domain.

### *Summary of Comparisons across Problems*

Summarizing cross-problem comparisons, the qualitative indicator of final theories and the quantitative indicator of prediction error yield slightly different results. As a result, there is no consistent evidence across indicators of differences in problem difficulty within the physical and social domains. Across domains, although final theories are less often correct in the social domain, this difference does not extend to prediction error. Analyses of strategies, to which we turn in Chapter V, will cast further light on the cross-domain comparison.

## KNOWLEDGE GAIN WITHIN PHASES

We turn now to an examination of knowledge gain within the first and second 5-week phases. Knowledge gain during a phase is examined irrespective of which problem a subject is working on within the physical or social domain. (Recall that half the subjects worked on the car problem during the first phase and the boat problem during the second phase while half worked on the problems in the reverse order. Problem order was similarly counterbalanced in the social domain.)

### *Theories*

Phase 1 results with respect to final theories (combined across car and boat problems in the physical domain and across school and TV problems in the social domain) closely parallel those reported earlier for both phases combined and hence need not be examined in detail. Subjects showed little difficulty confirming initial causal and noncausal theories. In the physical domain, 16 of 17 subjects offered correct final causal theories, and all 17 subjects did so in the social domain. In the case of noncausal theories, all 17 subjects were correct in the physical domain, and 15 of 17 were correct in the social domain.

With respect to the disconfirmation of a causal theory, however, results for the physical and social domains diverge, reflecting the same pattern apparent in Tables 2–5. In the physical domain, 15 of 17 subjects abandoned their incorrect causal theories (and expressed the correct noncausal theory). In the social domain, in contrast, only 4 of 17 subjects did so; the remainder continued to maintain that the feature was causal in their final theories.

Results for the more complex effects also are consistent with those reported in Tables 2–5. Four subjects discovered the interaction effect in the physical domain, compared to one subject in the social domain. The curvilinear effect was discovered by seven subjects in the physical domain and four in the social domain.

During phase 2, when subjects worked on the problems not worked on during phase 1, knowledge gains were comparable. In both the physical and the social domains, all 15 subjects who completed phase 2 confirmed their initially correct causal and noncausal theories. Subjects again exhibited difficulty, however, relinquishing incorrect causal theories in the social domain. Only five of 15 subjects did so in the social domain, compared to 12 of 15 in the physical domain. The interaction effect was discovered by five subjects in the physical domain and one in the social domain during phase 2, and the curvilinear effect was discovered by six subjects in the physical domain and seven in the social domain. There was thus no strong evidence of superior knowledge gain during phase 2.

### *Theory Stability*

Data on session-by-session change in theories offer insight into a subject's progress. They are best considered, however, in conjunction with an analysis of the evidence that a subject generated and the subject's strategies for interpreting it. We therefore postpone qualitative analysis of theory change, providing here only a quantitative indicator of the extent of theory stability. During their encounters with the two initial problems (phase 1), subjects changed their minds about a feature an average of 5.6 times in the physical domain and 4.7 times in the social domain—approximately one change of mind per session. For the second set of problems (phase 2), the figures are comparable, 4.9 changes of mind in the physical domain and 5.0 in the social domain. (These figures are based on three judgment possibilities—causal, noncausal, and "not sure.") Overall, then, theories were unstable across sessions, suggesting that knowledge gain did not occur in a smooth, incremental manner.

### *Prediction Error*

Knowledge gain during a phase can also be examined with respect to prediction error rate. In the physical domain, mean error rate during phase 1 decreased from .71 during the initial segment to .41 during the middle segment and remained comparable at .42 during the final segment. In the social domain, mean error rate decreased from .63 during the initial segment to .38 during the middle segment and rose again slightly to .46 during the final segment. Repeated-measures ANOVAs of these data showed a significant effect of time segment (initial, middle, and final; $F[2, 30] = 14.92$, $p < .001$). Effect of problem domain was not significant, nor was there a significant interaction. (The $N$ for this analysis was 16, as one subject was unable to make predictions in the social domain for the reason that he always selected instances based on outcome rather than feature combinations.) Since error rates decreased from initial to middle segments and then stabilized, a post hoc test for special contrasts using Dunn's *t*-test was performed on the data, showing no difference between middle and final segments but a significant difference between the initial segment and the average of the latter two segments ($t[15] = 5.15$, $p < .001$).

During phase 2, prediction error declined in a comparable way for the 15 subjects who completed phase 2—in the physical domain from .78 during the initial segment to .34 during the final segment and in the social domain from .64 in the initial segment to .39 in the final segment. Repeated-measures ANOVAs of prediction error for both phases combined yielded a significant effect of time segment ($F[5, 65] = 11.77$, $p < .001$), with no significant effect of problem domain and no interaction. Post hoc comparisons were comparable to those found for phase 1 data considered alone. Finally, comparison of the two phases shows no evidence of improved knowledge acquisition during phase 2.

## SUMMARY OF KNOWLEDGE ACQUISITION IN ADULTS

In summary, comparable results for the two phases with respect to both qualitative and quantitative indices show that knowledge of causal and noncausal effects increased during the time that subjects worked on a problem, although the quantitative index of error rate suggests that this progress was confined to the initial two-thirds of the time period. It should be kept in mind, however, that subjects tended to work on different aspects of the problem at different points in their investigation; for example, they considered more complex effects such as interactions only later in the investigation, after simple effects had been explored. Therefore, predictions may have become more difficult later in time, counteracting increases in skill level. Examination of strategies will shed further light both on this issue and on the suggestion from the qualitative data that relinquishing causal theories is more difficult in the social than in the physical domain.

# IV. KNOWLEDGE ACQUISITION IN CHILDREN

We turn now to an analysis of knowledge acquisition in the child sample. We examine the same two indicators we did for adults, the qualitative indicator of theory change and the quantitative indicator of outcome prediction. For each of these indicators, we also compare the performance of children and adults.

## COMPARISON ACROSS PROBLEMS

### *Theories*

A summary of subjects' initial and final theories for each of the four problems is presented in Tables 6–9. For most subjects, the first feature listed in each table involves the confirmation of an initially causal theory. A comparison with the first feature in the corresponding Tables 2–5 (Chap. III) for adult subjects shows that, despite slightly greater variability in initial theories among children, the children were only slightly less successful than the adults in recognizing the causal influence of this feature. Over all four problems, children's final theories were incorrect for this feature in a total of eight (of 58 possible) cases (compared to only one error of a possible 64 among adults). These errors appear to have been largely theory influenced; in six of the eight cases, the child's initial theory was also incorrect.

The second feature listed in Tables 6–9 most often involves the confirmation of an initially noncausal theory. When this is the case, as it almost always is for the problems in the physical domain (Tables 6 and 7), children perform almost as well as adults (although one child moved from a correct to an incorrect theory, which adults never did). In the social domain, however, approximately one-third of the initial theories for this feature are causal (making it more like the third feature in the tables), and children have difficulty recognizing its true noncausal status. As reflected in Table

TABLE 6

COMPARISON OF CHILDREN'S INITIAL AND FINAL THEORIES: CAR PROBLEM

| | THEORY | | |
|---|---|---|---|
| FEATURE | Initial | Final | Correctness |
| Engine size: | | | |
| Large > small | 12 | 12 | Correct |
| Small > large | 1 | 1 | |
| Noncausal | 2 | 2 | |
| Color: | | | |
| Blue > red | 1 | 1 | |
| Red > blue | 1 | 0 | |
| Noncausal | 13 | 14 | Correct |
| Muffler: | | | |
| On > off | 5 | 7 | |
| Off > on | 1 | 1 | |
| Noncausal | 8 | 6 | Correct |
| Don't know | 1 | 1 | |
| Fin: | | | |
| On > off | 2 | 1 | |
| Off > on | 2 | 8 | Partially correct |
| Noncausal | 10 | 4 | |
| Interaction (engine) | 0 | 0 | Correct |
| Don't know | 1 | 2 | |
| Wheel size: | | | |
| Small > med > large | 2 | 1 | |
| Small > large > med | 0 | 1 | |
| Small = med > large | 1 | 2 | |
| Large > med > small | 1 | 1 | |
| Large > small > med | 2 | 0 | |
| Med > small > large | 1 | 3 | Partially correct |
| Med > small = large | 1 | 3 | Correct |
| Noncausal | 7 | 3 | |
| Interaction (engine) | 0 | 1 | |

NOTE.—$N$ = 15. Entries refer to number of subjects reporting each type of theory at initial and final theory assessments.

9, incorrect theories for the second feature in the TV problem actually increase from initial to final assessment, accounted for by subjects who construct causal theories at some point subsequent to the initial assessment.

The third feature in the tables most often involves disconfirmation of an initial causal theory. Adults, recall, were largely successful in the physical domain but substantially less successful in the social domain, with no more than a third recognizing the correct noncausal status. Children, in contrast, show comparable difficulty in both domains. In the physical domain, only slightly more than a third recognize the feature's noncausal status; performance is comparable in the social domain, although the proportion rises to half for one of the problems.

TABLE 7

COMPARISON OF CHILDREN'S INITIAL AND FINAL THEORIES: BOAT PROBLEM

| Feature | Theory: Initial | Final | Correctness |
|---|---|---|---|
| Boat size: | | | |
| Small > large | 9 | 12 | Correct |
| Large > small | 3 | 1 | |
| Noncausal | 2 | 1 | |
| Sail color: | | | |
| Green > red | 0 | 0 | |
| Red > green | 0 | 1 | |
| Noncausal | 14 | 13 | Correct |
| Sail size: | | | |
| Large > small | 5 | 4 | |
| Small > large | 4 | 4 | |
| Noncausal | 5 | 5 | Correct |
| Interaction (boat size) | 0 | 1 | |
| Weight: | | | |
| On > off | 1 | 1 | |
| Off > on | 11 | 10 | Partially correct |
| Noncausal | 1 | 1 | |
| Interaction (boat size) | 0 | 1 | Correct |
| Interaction (boat size, but incorrect) | 1 | 1 | |
| Depth: | | | |
| Shallow > deep > med | 0 | 1 | |
| Shallow > med > deep | 2 | 2 | |
| Deep > med = shallow | 1 | 0 | |
| Deep > med > shallow | 4 | 5 | Partially correct |
| Deep = med > shallow | 0 | 1 | Correct |
| Noncausal | 7 | 2 | |
| Interaction (boat size) | 0 | 3 | |

NOTE.—$N$ = 14. One subject completed no sessions with the boat problem and was excluded.

Children also show less proficiency than adults in recognizing the causal status of a feature that they believe to be noncausal (which could occur for the first, fourth, or fifth features in Tables 6–9—the features that were in fact causal). In contrast to the adult sample, where the success rate ranged from 63% to 100% across problems, among cases in which an initial noncausal theory was held (a somewhat more common occurrence in the child sample) percentages of children who recognized the feature's causal status by the time of the final assessment ranged from 40% in the TV problem (six of the 15 subjects who held initial noncausal theories for one of the features that was in fact causal) to 60% in the boat problem (six of 10 subjects).

For the complex (interaction and curvilinear) effects, the picture is similarly one of knowledge acquisition moderately inferior to that of adults. Recognition of the correct curvilinear effect (which entails integration of

TABLE 8

COMPARISON OF CHILDREN'S INITIAL AND FINAL THEORIES: SCHOOL PROBLEM

| FEATURE | THEORY | | |
|---|---|---|---|
| | Initial | Final | Correctness |
| Teacher's assistant (TA): | | | |
| With TA > without TA | 8 | 13 | Correct |
| Without TA > with TA | 2 | 0 | |
| Noncausal | 4 | 1 | |
| Sex of principal: | | | |
| Female > male | 3 | 1 | |
| Male > female | 2 | 2 | |
| Noncausal | 9 | 11 | Correct |
| Noise in classroom: | | | |
| Quiet > noisy | 13 | 9 | |
| Noisy > quiet | 1 | 1 | |
| Noncausal | 0 | 4 | Correct |
| Teacher's activity during recess: | | | |
| Playground > lounge | 5 | 3 | |
| Lounge > playground | 2 | 4 | Partially correct |
| Noncausal | 7 | 7 | |
| Interaction (teacher's assistant) | 0 | 0 | Correct |
| Class size: | | | |
| Large > med > small | 4 | 1 | |
| Med > small = large | 1 | 0 | |
| Small = med > large | 0 | 1 | |
| Small > large > med | 0 | 1 | Partially correct |
| Small > med > large | 4 | 2 | Partially correct |
| Small > med = large | 1 | 4 | Correct |
| Noncausal | 4 | 5 | |

NOTE.—$N$ = 14. One subject completed no sessions with the school problem and was excluded.

causal and noncausal evidence) was achieved by only 7% (one subject) in the boat problem and rose to 29% in the school problem; intermediate percentages were 13% (TV problem) and 20% (car problem). (Percentages for adults, by comparison, ranged from 27% to 53% across problems.) Adults, recall, did poorly in recognition of the interaction effect; successes were near zero except for the boat problem, where 60% were successful. In the child sample, only one subject for one problem (boat) correctly recognized the interaction effect. Like adults, however, children do occasionally *theorize* interaction effects, as the tables show.

In sum, children perform almost as well as adults when knowledge acquisition is theory consonant (first and second features). In contrast, their performance drops below that of adults when the evidence is discrepant with an initial theory or when they are dealing with more complex (interactive or curvilinear) causal relations. In particular, children do not show the advantage that adults do in the physical over the social domain. In both

TABLE 9

COMPARISON OF CHILDREN'S INITIAL AND FINAL THEORIES: TV PROBLEM

| Feature | Theory: Initial | Final | Correctness |
|---|---|---|---|
| Music (M): | | | |
| With M > without M | 8 | 13 | Correct |
| Without M > with M | 2 | 0 | |
| Noncausal | 5 | 2 | |
| Day: | | | |
| Wed > Tu | 2 | 2 | |
| Tu > Wed | 3 | 5 | |
| Noncausal | 10 | 8 | Correct |
| Humor: | | | |
| Funny > serious | 13 | 7 | |
| Serious > funny | 0 | 0 | |
| Noncausal | 2 | 8 | Correct |
| Commercials (C): | | | |
| With C > without C | 2 | 7 | Partially correct |
| Without C > with C | 8 | 4 | |
| Noncausal | 5 | 4 | |
| Interaction (music) | 0 | 0 | Correct |
| Length (hours [h]): | | | |
| 2h > 1h > ½h | 5 | 2 | |
| 2h > 1h = ½h | 1 | 0 | |
| 1h > 2h > ½h | 1 | 0 | |
| 1h > ½h > 2h | 2 | 1 | |
| 1h > 2h = ½h | 0 | 1 | |
| ½h > 2h > 1h | 0 | 1 | Partially correct |
| ½h > 1h > 2h | 1 | 1 | Partially correct |
| ½h > 1h = 2h | 0 | 2 | Correct |
| Noncausal | 5 | 7 | |

NOTE.—$N$ = 15.

domains, children's performance is comparable to that of adults in the social domain.

*Prediction Error*

As in the analysis of the adult data, activity within each of the two phases was divided into initial, middle, and final segments to examine change over time. To compare prediction achievement across the four problems, prediction error rates for the final segment were calculated for each of the four problems, irrespective of whether a subject worked on this problem in phase 1 or phase 2.

Mean final segment error rates for problems in the physical domain were only slightly higher than those of adults—.46 (SD = .31) in the car problem and .49 (SD = .28) in the boat problem. (Corresponding percentages for adults were .42 and .33 for the car and boat problems, respectively.) In the social domain, however, performance fell well below that in the physical domain and well below that of adults—mean final segment error rates were .92 (SD = .40) in the school problem and .70 (SD = .33) in the TV problem. (Corresponding percentages for adults were .57 and .36 for the school and TV problems, respectively.)

### *Summary of Comparison across Problems*

Children show no notable differences across problems within domains, on either qualitative or quantitative indicators. Across the physical and social domains, they show no difference with respect to the qualitative indicator of final theory; as reflected in Tables 6–9, final theory errors are roughly equivalent across the four problems. Adults, in contrast, showed fewer final theory errors in the physical domain (compared to their own performance in the social domain and children's performance in both domains).

Across domains, in contrast, children do show a difference in predicting outcomes, with inferior performance in the social domain (compared to their own performance in the physical domain and adults' performance in both domains). Both age groups thus show some performance inferiority in the social domain but differ in the indicator in which this domain difference is reflected.

## KNOWLEDGE GAIN WITHIN PHASES

### *Theories*

A comparison of knowledge gain during the first and second 5-week phases (irrespective of which problem a subject worked on within the physical or social domain) reveals similar patterns. Children show equivalent theory change during the two phases. At each phase, their performance is almost as good as adults' when they are dealing with theory-consonant effects but drops below that of adults when they are dealing with theory-discrepant effects or when causal effects are more complex (interactive or curvilinear). Nor with respect to theory change do children during either phase show the superiority of performance in the physical domain that adults showed for both phases.

### *Theory Stability*

During phase 1, subjects changed their minds about a feature an average of 4.7 times in the physical domain and 4.8 times in the social domain (on the basis of three judgment possibilities—causal, noncausal, and "not sure")—approximately one change of mind per session. For phase 2, the figures are 4.4 in the physical domain and 2.9 in the social domain. (These and all subsequent comparisons in this chapter are based on an *N* of 15 for phase 1 and 14 for phase 2 since one subject did not complete phase 2.) These numbers are very close to those for adults except for the social domain during phase 2, where the lower variability reflects an increased faithfulness to largely incorrect theories. Strategy analysis will shed further light on these patterns.

### *Prediction Error*

Like adults, children show comparable prediction error patterns across phases. Recall, however, that, for adults, prediction error rates decreased across time for both phases and both domains. Children, in contrast, show improvement only in the physical domain; in the social domain, their error rates remain at a consistent level across the three segments of each phase. In the physical domain, during phase 1 mean error rate decreased from .77 during the initial segment to .66 during the middle segment and further declined to .48 during the final segment—error rates very similar to those of adults for the initial and final segments. Similarly during phase 2 in the physical domain, error rates were .84, .56, and .48 for the three segments, respectively, rates again similar to those of adults.

In the social domain, children's error rates were consistently higher than adults' and did not decline over time. During phase 1, they were .89, .70, and .85 for the three segments, respectively. During phase 2, they were .74, .66, and .76 for the three segments, respectively. Despite the indication of improved prediction in the physical domain, repeated-measures ANOVAs of children's prediction error data showed no effects of time for either phase separately or for the total period; an effect of domain reached significance only for the phase 1 analysis ($F[1, 14] = 5.20, p < .05$). No interactions of time and domain were significant.

## SUMMARY OF CHILDREN'S KNOWLEDGE ACQUISITION

Children, like adults, show increased knowledge of both causal and noncausal effects operating in a domain as a result of exploration within that domain. Differences in their knowledge acquisition, however, are evident. Summarizing across qualitative and quantitative indicators, children's performance falls below that of adults in a number of respects that involve both correctness of conclusions (final theories) and ability to predict outcomes.

Children's knowledge acquisition overall shows greater influence of theory than that of adults. For adults, this influence was most evident with respect to theories that were initially causal in the social domain. Among children, it extends across both physical and social domains and both initial causal and initial noncausal theories; in each of these cases, children's theoretical expectations appear to make it difficult for them to recognize theory-discrepant evidence. Finally, both age groups show some inferiority in the social, relative to the physical, domain. For adults, this difference is reflected qualitatively in the correctness of final theories; for children, it is reflected in the quantitative indicator of prediction error.

The analyses presented in this and the preceding chapter are limited by the fact that knowledge acquisition is best understood in the context of the strategies by means of which it is acquired. As we will see, children's strategies and strategy change differ from adults' in a number of respects, and we need to consider knowledge acquisition in this light. We turn, therefore, to the strategies that both adults and children used to acquire their improved knowledge.

# V. STRATEGIES AND STRATEGY CHANGE IN ADULTS

How did adult subjects achieve their increased knowledge of the domains that they examined? We first examine strategies and strategy change during phase 1 only. We then turn to phase 2 results in examining the issue of transfer when subjects switch to new problems in each domain.

## INVESTIGATIVE STRATEGIES

The ultimate indicator on which we rely in judging the success of subjects' strategies is the validity of their inferences. However, several additional indicators having to do with the nature of investigative processes are informative, and we consider these first.

### *Problem Space Investigated*

One such indicator is how much of the problem space is investigated. For each problem, the number of unique combinations of features is 48. The mean number of instances that subjects generated was 24.3 in the physical and 23.3 in the social domain. Generating this number of instances, it would have been possible to investigate only roughly 50% of the problem space. However, not all the instances generated were unique (some were replications). The mean number of *unique* instances that subjects generated was 16.6 in the physical domain (range 10–23) and 16.4 in the social (range 10–22). Hence, only about one-third of the problem space was investigated in each of the domains. The implication is that inefficient investigation of the problem space reduced the information that subjects had access to, with some subjects working with a very limited database of as few as 10 unique instances.

### *Investigative Intent*

The appropriateness of the evidence that is generated must be judged relative to a subject's investigative intent. During phase 1, subjects' investigative intents became more focused; they less often expressed the intent to assess the effects of multiple features by examining a single instance or pair of instances. In the physical domain, the mean number of features referred to in response to the intent inquiry ("Which features are you trying to find out about?") was 1.56 (range 1.00–2.80) during the initial segment, 1.51 during the middle segment (range 1.00–2.38), and 1.38 in the final segment (range 1.00–1.90). In the social domain, comparable means were 2.20 (range 1.10–3.40), 2.02 (range 1.00–4.00), and 1.75 (range 1.00–4.20) for the three segments, respectively. The time-period effect was significant ($F[2, 32] = 5.01, p < .05$), as was the problem domain (physical vs. social; $F[1, 16] = 7.96, p < .05$), with no significant interaction. Post hoc tests using Scheffé's procedure showed a significant difference between middle and final segments but not between initial and middle segments.

In sum, performance with respect to focus of investigative intent was overall inferior in the social domain but showed comparable improvement during phase 1 in both domains. In considering these numbers, it should be kept in mind that an index of 1.00 does not necessarily represent normative or ideal performance since, in the latter segments, a subject's intent may have been to investigate interactions between features. Nonetheless, despite this influence (which would lead the index to increase), overall it decreased over time.

### *Coordination of Intent and Inference*

Do subjects in fact draw inferences regarding the features that they state an intention to investigate? This coordination between intent and inference is a further index of the quality of investigative activity. To assess the level of this coordination, the number of stated intents to investigate a feature that were followed by a corresponding inference regarding that feature was compared to the total number of intents. In the physical domain, the resulting proportions across subjects were .70 during the initial segment, .81 during the middle segment, and .81 during the final segment. In the social domain, the corresponding means were .58, .73, and .78, respectively. The effect of time period was significant ($F[2, 32] = 7.46, p < .01$), with no significant effect of problem domain and no significant interaction. Post hoc Scheffé tests showed only the difference between the first two segments to be significant. Coordination of intent and inference was thus roughly comparable across the two domains and with time improved to a fairly high, but less than perfect, level.

### *Multiple-Instance Evidence*

Do subjects generate evidence that is adequate to allow the inferences that they wish to make? Specifically, do they recognize that a comparison of at least two instances is necessary to permit an inference regarding the effect of a feature? To address this question, the number of inferences based on two or more instances (compared to those based on a single instance) was compared to the total number of inferences that the subject made. In the physical domain, the mean of these ratios across subjects was .76 during the initial segment, .87 during the middle segment, and .92 during the final segment. In the social domain, the corresponding means were .54, .72, and .86, respectively. The time-period effect was significant ($F[2, 32] = 10.01$, $p < .01$), as was problem domain ($F[1, 16] = 6.67$, $p < .05$), with no significant interaction. Post hoc tests using Dunn's procedure (used because the local sphericity assumption was violated) showed significant differences between initial and middle and between middle and final segments. Use of multiple-instance evidence, like coordination of intent and inference, thus improved with time to a fairly high, although less than perfect, level, with slight superiority in the physical domain.

### *Summary of Investigative Strategies*

In sum, although subjects did not optimize their opportunity to access the evidence base available to them (as assessed by the percentage of problem space investigated), the preceding indicators reflect significant improvement in investigative competence across the first phase of investigative activity. For the two indicators in which performance differed significantly across problem domains, performance was superior in the physical domain. However, the consistent lack of interaction between problem domain and time period indicates that improvement was comparable across domains.

## INFERENCE

In the course of their investigations, subjects were free to make as many or as few inferences as they wished. Each determinate inference (i.e., a judgment that a feature did or did not make a difference) that a subject made was coded as to its validity. (Indeterminate inferences—e.g., "I can't tell if color matters" or "It might make a difference"—were not coded.) The basis for this assessment was the response to the justification question ("How do you know that ——— makes a/no difference?"). If the subject made no reference to evidence (the justification being entirely theory based), the inference was coded as invalid. If the subject did make reference to evidence that was either present at that point or had been generated previously, the evidence referred to was assessed as adequate or inadequate to justify the inference. In order for the evidence to be judged adequate and the inference therefore valid, the subject needed to refer to at least two instances in which the focal feature varied and all other features remained constant. Finally, for the inference to be judged valid, the subject needed in addition to draw the appropriate inference, that is, inclusion if the outcome varied and exclusion if it did not. Valid and invalid inferences were further categorized into types (to be described later). Ten percent of the total set of inferences were coded independently by two of the authors, with intercoder agreement of 97%. The remaining inferences were coded by one of the authors.

Subjects made more inferences in the social domain (a mean of 40.06 per problem across subjects for the five sessions combined, compared to 32.80 in the physical domain). However, the proportion of inferences that were valid was higher in the physical domain, as seen in Figure 1. Despite this domain difference in validity, validity of inferences increased across time to a comparable degree in the two domains (Fig. 1). The domain difference was significant ($F[1, 16] = 11.19, p < .01$), as was the time-period effect ($F[2, 32] = 23.52, p < .001$), with no significant interaction.

It is important to supplement this overall portrayal of inferential competence and change over time with qualitative data on individual patterns, particularly with respect to initial and terminal competence. Examining inferences based on just the first two instances that a subject generated (since it is only after two instances have been generated that a valid inference becomes possible), a picture emerges of at least some initial inferential competence in many subjects. Two of the 17 subjects made at least one valid inference on the basis of the first two instances that they generated, in both the physical and the social problems. Six of 17 made a valid inference in either the physical or the social problem, but not both. By the end of the first session, a total of 10 subjects had made at least one valid inference in one of the problems. This number had risen to 14 by the end of the first segment of phase 1 and to 16 by the end of phase 1. It should be kept in mind, however, that all subjects continued to make invalid inferences during this period. Consistent with the significant domain effect, initial valid inferences were more likely to be in the physical domain.

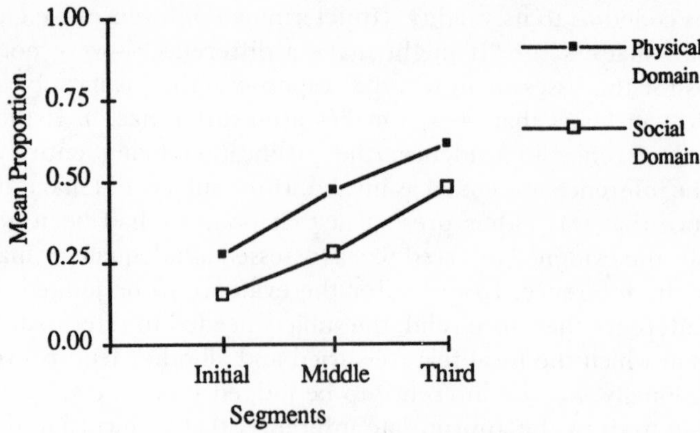


FIG. 1.—Proportion of valid inferences for the adult sample, phase 1 ($N = 17$)

## TRANSFER TO PHASE 2

Was the increased competence in investigation and inference that subjects manifested during phase 1 maintained when new problem content was introduced at the onset of phase 2? Did this competence further increase during phase 2? To answer these questions, three a priori contrasts were designed, comparing performance during specific segments of phase 1 (segments 1–3) and phase 2 (segments 4–6). The first comparison is between segments 1 and 4, assessing whether initial performance in phase 2 was higher or lower than initial performance in phase 1. The second comparison is between segments 3 and 6, assessing whether the final level attained in phase 2 exceeded that attained in phase 1. The third comparison is between segments 3 and 4, assessing whether the switch to new problem content beginning with segment 4 led to a decrement in performance.

### *Problem Space Investigated*

We begin with the one indicator that does not lend itself to specific comparisons across segments—the overall percentage of problem space investigated. Yet the possibility exists that, by phase 2, subjects become more aware of the size of the problem space and may generate a larger number of unique instances. A repeated-measures ANOVA conducted across both phases, however, showed no significant effects of phase or domain on number of unique instances generated (of the possible 48). For the 15 subjects completing both phases, these means were 16.7 and 16.1 in phase 1, for the physical and social domains, respectively. In phase 2, the comparable means were 15.7 and 18.0, respectively. Hence, the percentage of problem space investigated remained fairly constant at about one-third.

### *Investigative Intent*

For the 15 subjects completing both phases, mean number of features referred to in response to the intent inquiry, which declined significantly during phase 1, did not change significantly with the introduction of phase 2. For these subjects, the mean was 1.37 for segment 3 and 1.41 for segment 4 in the physical domain and 1.70 for segment 3 and 1.85 for segment 4 in the social domain. The contrasts between segments 3 and 6 were marginally significant ($t[14] = 2.21, p < .05$), with means of 1.20 and 1.30 for segment 6 in the physical and social domains, respectively, indicating continued improvement during phase 2. (Because the local sphericity assumption was violated, this and several subsequent contrasts were performed using Dunn's *t*-test.) The contrast between segments 1 and 4 did not reach statistical significance, despite an overall significant effect of time ($F[5, 70] = 5.43$, $p < .01$) as well as of problem domain ($F[1, 14] = 6.00, p < .01$)—the latter indicating continuing superiority in the physical domain.

### *Coordination of Intent and Inference*

Recall that intents and inferences became more coordinated during phase 1, with increasingly greater proportions of stated intents to investigate a feature followed by a corresponding inference regarding that feature. These proportions did not change significantly with the introduction of phase 2. For the 15 subjects completing both phases, the means were .80 and .81 in the physical domain and .78 and .82 in the social domain for segments 3 and 4, respectively. Contrasts between segments 3 and 6 were again marginally significant ($F[1, 14] = 5.07$, $p < .05$), with segment 6 means of .90 and .86 in the physical and social domains, respectively, indicating continued improvement during phase 2. The contrast between segments 1 and 4 was also significant ($F[1, 14] = 12.60, p < .05$), as was the overall effect of time ($F[5, 70] = 6.88, p < .001$), with no significant effect of domain and no interaction.

### *Multiple-Instance Evidence*

During phase 1, subjects made increasing use of at least two instances as a basis for an inference. Proportion of multiple-instance inferences did not change significantly with the introduction of phase 2. For the 15 subjects completing both phases, the means were .98 and .94 in the physical domain

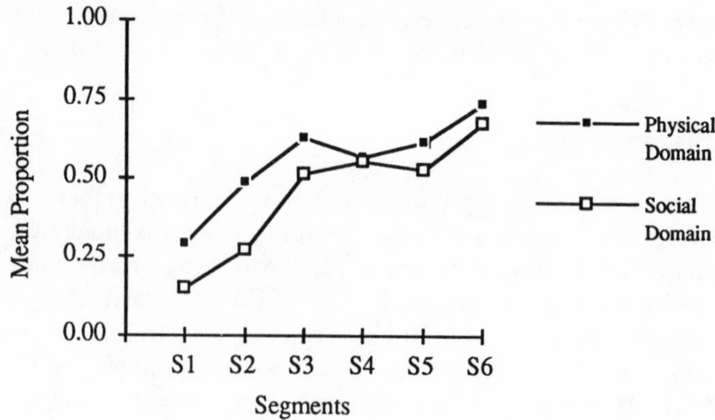


FIG. 2.—Proportion of valid inferences for the adult sample, phases 1 and 2 ($N = 15$).

and .90 and .83 in the social domain for segments 3 and 4, respectively. Means for segment 6 were .99 and .90 in the physical and social domains, respectively, not significantly different from segment 3 and thus indicating no continued improvement. The contrast between segment 1 (with means of .82 and .57, respectively, in the two domains) and segment 4 was significant ($t[14] = 3.62$, $p < .05$), as was the overall effect of time ($F[5, 70] = 8.94$, $p < .05$) and problem domain ($F[1, 14] = 5.27$, $p < .05$)—the latter indicating a continued slight superiority in the physical domain.

### *Inference*

The major indicator on which we rely in assessing transfer is validity of inferences. The results are displayed in Figure 2 for the 15 subjects who completed both phases. As Figure 2 reflects, there was no decline in level of validity of inferences from segment 3 to segment 4. In contrast, the difference between segments 1 and 4 was significant ($t[14] = 4.04$, $p < .01$) and between segments 3 and 6 marginally significant ($t[14] = 2.14$, $p < .05$), indicating continued improvement during phase 2. Overall effect of time was significant ($F[5, 70] = 17.20$, $p < .01$), as was the superiority of performance in the physical domain ($F[1, 14] = 7.41$, $p < .05$), with no interaction.

Analysis of individual patterns shows that, by segment 6, all subjects had shown at least some valid inference. Four subjects had attained levels of valid inference of 100% in the physical domain, and five had done so in the social domain (compared to only three subjects in each domain at the end of phase 1). The remaining majority of subjects continued to exhibit invalid as well as valid inferences.

### *Summary of Transfer Results*

The preceding results indicate clearly that the progress in strategies of investigation and inference that was observed during phase 1 was not compromised by the introduction of new content during phase 2. Depending on the particular indicator, strategies either were maintained at their current level or continued to improve during phase 2.

## THE NATURE AND USE OF INFERENCE STRATEGIES

The major purpose of the transfer design was to establish that the inference strategies examined here have some generality across a wide range of content. Establishing the generality of these strategies enhances their significance and justifies further analysis of their nature, the relations that they bear to one another, and the ways in which they are applied. It is to this analysis that we now turn.

### *Overall Quantity and Validity of Inclusion and Exclusion Inferences*

The problem format, recall, allowed subjects to make as many or as few inferences as they wished, and these could be of any type the subject wished. As shown in Figure 3, subjects made more inferences of inclusion (judgments that a feature was causal) than exclusion (judgments that a feature was noncausal) ($F[1, 14] = 34.76$, $p < .001$). They also made more inferences overall in the social domain than they did in the physical ($F[1, 14] = 4.92$, $p < .05$). The difference between number of inclusion and exclusion inferences is greater in the social domain and greater in phase 1, owing to an increased number of inclusion inferences in the social domain in phase 1. The interaction between inference type and problem domain reached statistical significance ($F[1, 14] = 7.02$, $p < .05$), whereas the interaction between inference type and time did not. Although inclusion inferences decreased from phase 1 to phase 2 (mainly in the social domain), as reflected in Figure 3, there was neither a significant main effect nor any interactions involving time.

Analysis of the validity of inclusion and exclusion inferences considered separately shows consistently lower validity rates for inclusion inferences. During phase 1 in the physical domain, the mean proportion of valid inclu-

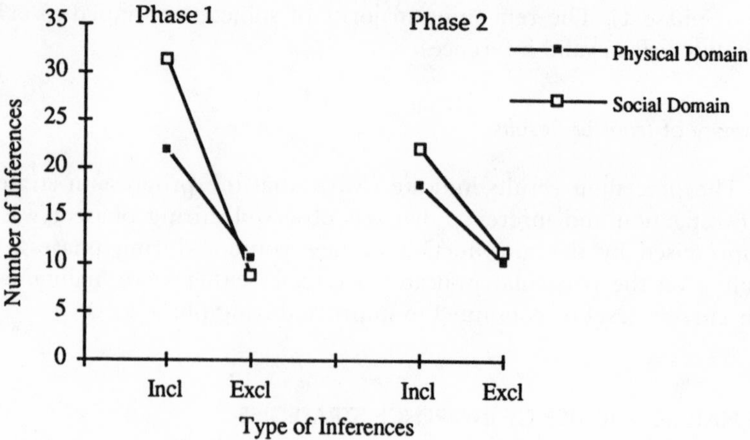


FIG. 3.—Mean number of inferences by phase, problem domain, and inference type, for the adult sample.

sion inferences was .43, compared to .76 for valid exclusion inferences. In the social domain, the mean proportion of valid inclusion inferences was an even lower .27, compared to .72 for exclusion. Validity improves overall during phase 2, as noted earlier, but differences in validity rates for inclusion and exclusion remain at phase 2: .63 for inclusion and .79 for exclusion in the physical domain and .50 for inclusion and .90 for exclusion in the social domain.

Overall, then, subjects were more likely to make inferences of inclusion than of exclusion, but inclusion inferences were less likely to be valid. The final (segment 6) validity rate of exclusion was near ceiling (.86 and 1.00 in the physical and social domains, respectively), compared to the more modest achievement in validity of inclusion inferences (segment 6 rates of .73 and .57 in the physical and social domains, respectively).

### *False Inclusion*

The logic of valid inclusion and exclusion inferences is straightforward. More interesting is the form that subjects' invalid inferences take. What forms of erroneous justification do subjects use for claiming that a feature is causal or noncausal? We begin with inclusion. One reason that inclusion inferences could have been invalid was that they made no reference to evidence, even after probing. During phase 1, 10% of inclusion inferences fell into this category of *theory-based* inferences. During phase 2, this percentage diminished to 3%.

When inclusion inferences did make reference to evidence, a number of different inferential errors were exhibited. As described in Chapter I, the *co-occurrence* false inclusion inference is based on a single instance (in which a particular level of a feature and outcome co-occur), leading the subject to conclude that the feature played a causal role in the outcome. Analyses presented earlier in this chapter indicate that single-instance inferences were common initially; during segment 1, 24% and 46% of inferences in the physical and social domains, respectively, were single instance (and predominantly evidence based). These inferences, however, became uncommon with time. (By segment 6, 99% and 90% of inferences in the physical and social domains, respectively, were multiple-instance inferences, as reported earlier.) Thus, once an evidence base of multiple instances has been generated, it becomes likely that a subject will draw on a comparison of at least two instances as the basis for an inference.

Multiple-instance false inclusion inferences are most likely to be of the *covariation* form described in Chapter I, in which levels of a feature and an outcome covary over two or more instances, but with the influence of additional features uncontrolled. In addition, the *generalized* inclusion inferences described in Chapter I were included in this category. Generalized inclusion inferences composed a noteworthy, but not major, portion of the total in this category—7% in the physical and 6% in the social domain. As explained earlier, these inferences can be, and in fact often were, incorrect, for one of two reasons—either because the database of instances generated by the subject is not representative of the true population of instances, a situation that accounted for 12% of generalized inclusion inferences in the physical and 26% in the social domain, or because the subject incorrectly represents the database that has been generated, accounting for 24% of generalized inclusion inferences in the physical and 33% in the social domain. The remaining generalized inclusion inferences (64% in the physical domain and 42% in the social domain) were factually correct, that is, true characterizations of the causal structure, even though the subject had not generated a valid comparison of instances to demonstrate the alleged effect. As these percentages reflect, errors were greater in the social domain; that is, subjects were more likely to misuse generalized inclusion inference to reach incorrect conclusions in the social domain.

### *False Exclusion*

In contrast to false inclusion inferences, which were the most prevalent inference form overall, false exclusion inferences were the least prevalent (as reflected in the previously reported greater frequencies of inclusion over exclusion inferences and valid over invalid exclusion inferences). As anticipated (see Chap. I), generalized exclusion inferences were rare. A total of nine such inferences were observed—six in the physical domain and three in the social. Of these, four of the six were correct in the physical domain and one of the three in the social domain, reflecting the same higher error rate in the social domain as observed in the case of generalized inclusion inferences.

Although false exclusion inferences were relatively infrequent overall, a variety of types appeared. The most common reason that exclusion inferences were invalid is that they did not reference the data. During phase 1, 21% of all false exclusion inferences were entirely theory based, and this percentage remained comparable (23%) during phase 2—higher, note, than the percentage of theory-based inclusion inferences and reflecting the fact that subjects were more likely to fail to investigate features believed noncausal (a result to be examined further shortly).

As in the case of inclusion, some evidence-based false exclusion inferences were based on only a single instance, with the subject claiming, for example, "The fin makes no difference because this car has it and [still] went fast." False exclusion based on multiple instances could take a number of forms. In some cases, the excluded feature did not vary across the instances being compared (e.g., "Sail size makes no difference because both boats had large sails and one got only to the third flag and the other got to the fourth"). In other cases in which the excluded feature did vary, other factors were left uncontrolled (and hence could exert their own effects on the outcome). Or a subject may have justified an exclusion by appealing to effects of other features (e.g., "The muffler doesn't matter because it's the size of the engine that's making the difference").

### *Valid Inclusion and Exclusion*

Valid inclusion and exclusion inferences occurred when the subject drew the appropriate inference that followed from a controlled comparison—inclusion if the outcomes differed in correspondence with the manipulated feature, exclusion if they did not. As noted earlier, all subjects had shown some valid inference by segment 6 (and almost all by segment 3). For all subjects, these valid inferences included both inclusion and exclusion. Thus, even though they may not have used it consistently, all subjects had competence in the basic forms of valid inference.

One question that might be raised regarding the controlled comparisons on which valid inferences are based is whether they were intended, and the answer is largely yes. In roughly 80% of cases—a percentage that remained fairly constant across all six segments—in advance of actually viewing the data the subject stated an intent to investigate the role of the manipulated feature, and only that feature. Thus, the comparisons that led to valid inferences were largely intended. More difficult to discern with certainty, however, is whether the *control* aspect of the comparison was intended. The likelihood is small that the four remaining features that were not the focus of the comparison would be held constant without the intention to do so, although such "accidental" control could have been involved in some small proportion of valid inferences. It does not follow, however, that subjects who did intentionally hold other features constant in making a comparison understood the significance of doing so. We return to this issue in the concluding chapter.

Although competently executed in establishing the causal or noncausal role of a particular feature, few valid inferences reflected any concern with second-order (interaction) effects, that is, any indication of the possibility that the effect or lack thereof that had been identified might be limited to the particular levels of other features for which it had been demonstrated and/or might not appear at other levels of these features. For example, a subject might conclude, "For the small classes, noise makes no difference," suggesting at least implicitly the possibility that the result could be different for larger classes. The percentage of valid inferences that were qualified in this way remained fairly constant at about 8%–10%, across time, across domains, and across inclusion versus exclusion. It should be noted, however, that this same percentage of 8%–10% also held true for invalid inferences. Thus, the ability to make controlled comparisons and draw valid conclusions regarding simple causal and noncausal effects did not appear to enhance awareness of the possibility of second-order effects.

The number of cases in which a subject actually generated and correctly interpreted the evidence needed to demonstrate an interaction between two features is even smaller. A minimum of four instances is required—two to demonstrate the presence/absence of an effect at one level of a second feature and two more to assess whether the presence (or absence) of this effect holds at a contrasting level of the second feature, with all remaining features held constant across these comparisons. In the physical domain, seven subjects correctly demonstrated the presence or absence of nine interactions. In the social domain, there occurred only one correct demonstration of the absence of an interaction.

### *Patterns of Change for Inference Types Considered Individually*

An analysis of change in validity rates over time for inclusion and exclusion considered individually yielded results similar to those reported earlier for total inferences. For inclusion, differences between segments 3 and 4 and between 3 and 6 were not significant, in contrast to a significant difference between segments 1 and 4 ($t[14] = 4.50$, $p < .01$), and overall effect of time was significant ($F[5, 70] = 12.30, p < .01$), as was the superiority of performance in the physical domain ($F[1, 14] = 19.28, p < .001$). A comparable statistical analysis for exclusion could not be performed since eight subjects made no exclusion inferences in at least one segment. However, the validity rate of exclusion inferences shows the same overall pattern of improvement during phase 1 and maintenance of this improved rate during phase 2, particularly in the social domain, where performance is lower overall and there is more room for improvement—validity of exclusion in the social domain improved from .48 during segment 1 to .92 during segment 3 (compared to improvement from .64 to .85 in the physical domain).

It is also informative to consider trends over time with respect to the absolute numbers of inferences of the various types. In the case of exclusion, overall improvement in validity was contributed to about equally by trends of both types—decline in the number of false exclusion and increase in the number of valid exclusion inferences. In the case of inclusion, however, increases in the number of valid inferences were relatively small—a mean increase of between one and two inferences from phase 1 to phase 2. A much greater proportion of the improvement in validity rate was contributed to by a decline in the number of false inclusion inferences—a mean decline of 5.64 inferences from phase 1 to phase 2 in the physical domain and an even more dramatic mean decline of 10.88 inferences in the social domain.

In sum, the major improvement over time in inclusion is in the inhibition of false inclusion inferences. Still, as noted earlier, invalid inference, and specifically invalid inclusion, far from disappears and continues to be exhibited by a majority of subjects. Of the 11 of 15 subjects in the physical domain and the 10 of 15 in the social domain reported earlier as continuing to show invalid inference, some did not continue to show invalid exclusion (which, recall, had a low overall rate of occurrence) during the latter portions of their performance, but all continued to exhibit false inclusion.

### *The Influence of Theory on Investigation and Inference*

The primary way in which we will examine the influence of subjects' theories on their investigation and interpretation of evidence is by the qualitative analysis of individual patterns of performance. However, several quantitative indicators document the influence of subjects' theories on their investigation and inference. At one extreme are inferences that were entirely theory based, that is, that did not make reference to evidence at all, even in response to probes. These frequencies were reported earlier. Even when subjects' inferences did draw on the evidence base, however, the in-

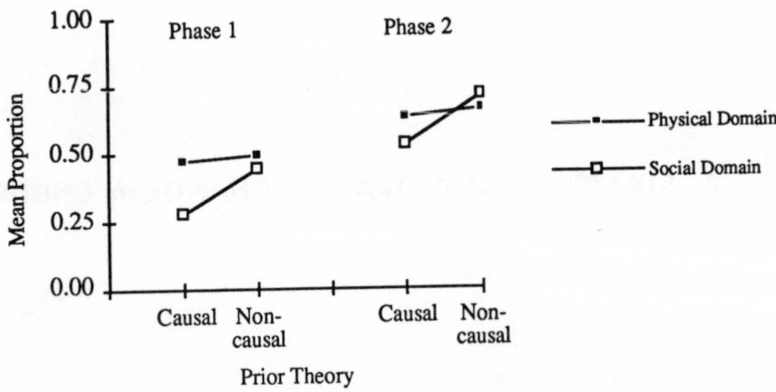


FIG. 4.—Proportion of valid inferences as a function of theoretical belief, for the adult sample.

fluence of their theories by no means disappears. Subjects paid more attention to features that they believed to be causal than to features they believed noncausal. This difference was reflected both in the number of times a feature was mentioned in statements of intent to investigate and the number of times an inference was actually made regarding that feature. For intent, the theory effect was significant ($F[1, 14] = 122.95$, $p < .001$), with no effects of phase or domain. For inferences, the theory effect was likewise significant ($F[1, 14] = 95.75$, $p < .001$) and consistent across phases and domains. (The theory status—causal or noncausal—of an intent or inference in these analyses was based on the theory assessment that took place at the immediately preceding session.)

The influence of theory extends to the validity of inferences. Although subjects attended more to features they believed causal, the inferences made about features believed noncausal were more likely to be valid. As reflected in Figure 4, this difference is focused in the social domain. In addition to a significant effect of theory ($F[1, 14] = 8.44$, $p < .05$) was the interaction between theory and domain ($F[1, 14] = 6.27$, $p < .05$), with the theory effect focused in the social domain. As seen in Figure 4, this interaction primarily reflects the diminished validity of inferences in the social domain for features believed causal. This finding is consonant with the data on final conclusions presented in Tables 2–5 above, indicating that subjects found it hardest to relinquish causal theories in the social domain. We return to this finding in examining qualitative data.

# VI. STRATEGIES AND STRATEGY CHANGE IN CHILDREN

In this chapter, we examine the strategies that children used to achieve their increased knowledge and how these strategies changed over time with use. In both respects, we compare children's performance to that of adults. Of particular interest are any strategic differences that might help explain children's less effective knowledge acquisition. Contrary to the way in which data were presented for adults, however, we present results for both phase 1 and phase 2 at the same time, for each of the indicators. We therefore examine questions of initial performance, improvement during phase 1, and transfer to phase 2 together for each indicator as well as comparing results to those for adults in each of these respects.

## INVESTIGATIVE STRATEGIES

### *Problem Space Investigated*

*Phase 1.*—The 15 children who completed phase 1 generated a mean of 22.2 instances (of a possible 48) in the physical domain and 21.2 instances in the social domain, numbers very close to those for adults. The mean number of unique instances generated was 16.0 in the physical domain (range 13–19) and 14.6 in the social domain (range 11–19), numbers again very close to those for adults. Thus, children did not access as much of the database as they might have, averaging only about one-third, but their performance was not inferior to adults' in this respect.

*Phase 2.*—For the 14 subjects completing both phases, mean number of unique instances (as well as total instances) did not change greatly during phase 2. Phase 2 means were 14.4 in the physical domain and 13.7 in the social domain (compared to phase 1 means of 15.9 and 14.6, respectively, for these 14 subjects). A repeated-measures ANOVA covering both phases showed no significant effect of phase or domain on number of unique instances generated. Thus, as was the case for adults, efficient investigation of the problem space showed no improvement during phase 2, and subjects worked throughout with only a limited portion of the potential database.

### *Investigative Intent*

*Phase 1.*—Like adults, children during phase 1 became more focused over time with respect to the features they intended to find out about, increasingly less often expressing an intent to assess effects of multiple features by examining a single instance or pair of instances. In the physical domain, the mean number of features referred to in response to the intent inquiry ("Which features are you trying to find out about?") was 1.89 (range .86–3.00) during the initial segment, 1.56 during the middle segment (range .88–3.14), and 1.41 during the final segment (range .71–2.57). In the social domain, means were 2.48 (range .71–4.43), 1.93 (range .63–4.00), and 1.51 (range .43–3.29), for the three segments, respectively. An effect of time period was significant ($F[2, 28] = 10.78, p < .001$), as was domain ($F[1, 14] = 7.76, p < .05$), with no significant interaction. Scheffé post hoc tests showed significant differences only between initial and final segments. Compared to adults, children showed slight inferiority in the initial segment in both domains and slight superiority in the final segment in the social domain. Otherwise, their performance was very close to that of adults, with both age groups showing improvement in focusing investigative intent but inferiority in the social domain.

*Phase 2.*—As was the case for adults, children's means did not change significantly with the introduction of phase 2 (segment 4). In the physical domain, the mean was 1.41 for segment 3 and 1.35 for segment 4 (for the 14 subjects completing both phases); in the social domain, it was 1.52 for segment 3 and 1.38 for segment 4. By segment 6, these means had declined to 1.19 and 1.20 for the physical and social domains, respectively, close to the segment 6 means for adults. Contrasts between segments 3 and 4 and between segments 3 and 6 were nonsignificant, but the contrast between segments 1 and 4 reached significance ($F[1, 13] = 18.25, p < .001$), reflecting improvement during phase 1. In contrast to adults, then, children showed no continued improvement during phase 2. Overall the effect of time was significant ($F[5, 65] = 9.36, p < .001$), but the effect of domain did not reach significance (whereas it did for adults).

### *Coordination of Intent and Inference*

*Phase 1.*—To assess coordination of intent and inference, the number of stated intents to investigate a feature that were followed by a corresponding inference regarding that feature was compared to the total number of intents. The resulting proportions in the physical domain were .67 during the initial segment, .68 during the middle segment, and .75 during the final segment. In the social domain, they were .69, .71, and .70 in the three segments, respectively. These proportions were in the same range as those for adults but showed less improvement over time, and there were no significant effects of either time or domain.

*Phase 2.*—During phase 2, degree of coordination of intent and inference remained at roughly its phase 1 level. No statistical effects emerged for time or domain. In the physical domain, the proportion of inferences coordinated with an intent dropped slightly to .69 during segment 4 (from a segment 3 level of .76 for the 14 subjects completing phase 2) and then rose to .82 by segment 6. In the social domain, the proportion was .67 during segment 4 (compared to a segment 3 level of .69 for the 14 subjects completing phase 2) and similarly was still at .70 during segment 6. These segment 6 proportions are slightly below those for adults (.90 and .86 in the physical and social domains, respectively), who, recall, continued to show significant improvement during phase 2. In contrast to adults, then, children did not improve significantly in coordination of intent and inference, but, as was the case for adults, there was no evidence of inferiority in the social domain.

### *Multiple-Instance Evidence*

*Phase 1.*—The proportion of inferences based on at least two instances—the minimum necessary for valid inference—was calculated across segments and domains for each subject. In the physical domain, the mean proportion across subjects was .58 during the initial segment, .47 during the middle segment, and .49 during the final segment. In the social domain, these means were .23, .38, and .48, respectively. Statistical analyses showed no effect of time period, an effect of domain ($F[1, 14] = 4.74$, $p < .05$), and a significant interaction between time and domain ($F[2, 28] = 4.93$, $p < .05$). This performance was consistently below that of adults (who showed significant improvement in both domains to segment 3 levels of .92 in the physical and .86 in the social domain). Children, in contrast, showed improvement only in one domain, and, even by the third segment, at most a single instance provided the basis for an inference in over half the inferences in both domains. Like adults, however, their performance was superior in the physical domain.

*Phase 2.*—During phase 2, children's performance is very similar. In the physical domain, the proportion of multiple-instance inferences remained at .49 during segment 4 (identical to the .49 during segment 3 for the 14 subjects completing both phases) and was still .49 by segment 6. In the social domain, the proportion was .28 during segment 4 and had improved to .47 by segment 6, a pattern almost identical to the phase 1 pattern and one suggesting some relearning in this domain with the introduction of new content. No individual contrasts were significant. The interaction between domain and time was significant ($F[5, 65] = 3.08, p < .05$), as was the effect of domain ($F[1, 13] = 5.06, p < .05$), but there was no overall effect of time. Failure to draw on multiple-instance evidence thus continued to be a problem for children during phase 2; performance also continued to be inferior in the social domain.

### *Summary of Investigative Strategies*

In sum, despite their less effective knowledge acquisition observed in Chapter IV, children showed investigative strategies almost equivalent to those of adults, except with respect to the use of multiple-instance evidence. These strategic abilities—maximizing investigation of the problem space, appropriate investigative intent, coordination of intent and inference, and appropriate use of evidence as a basis for inference—are far from perfectly exhibited among adults, as we saw in the preceding chapter. A particular weakness on the part of children, however, appears to be the appropriate use of multiple-instance evidence. We return to this characteristic in examining qualitative data. We also return to the inferiority in the social domain exhibited by both age groups.

## INFERENCE

### *Phase 1*

Each determinate inference that a child made was coded as described in Chapter V for adults. As might be anticipated from the comparatively low frequencies of multiple-instance evidence, children's inferences were less often valid than those of adults. The proportions of inferences that were valid during phase 1 are shown in the first half of Figure 5. (Figure 5 is based on the 14 subjects who completed both phases, but the percentages are very similar when the additional subject who completed only phase 1 is included.) The time effect was significant ($F[2, 28] = 8.68, p < .001$), as was domain ($F[1, 14] = 5.65, p < .05$), with no interaction. Like adults, children show superiority in the physical domain. However, level of validity

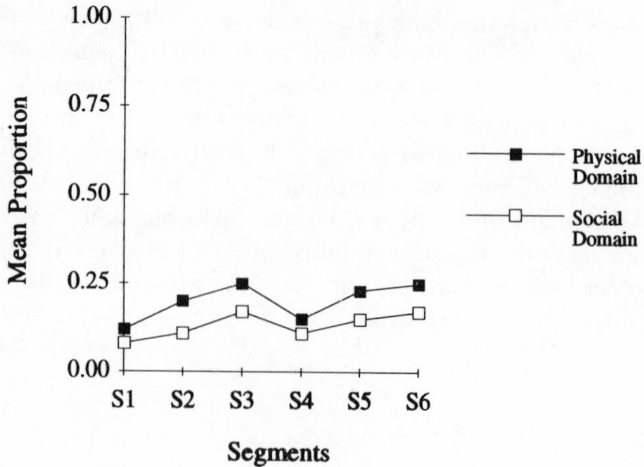


FIG. 5.—Proportion of valid inferences for the child sample, phases 1 and 2 ($N$ = 14).

of inferences was substantially lower than that shown by adults, at both initial and final segments.

The differences between the child and the adult samples in this respect are best examined qualitatively. Initial inferential competence of the children is overall lower than that of the adults but also more variable. Most adults, recall, showed some initial competence within the first one or two sessions but continued to show invalid strategies as well throughout the period of observation. Of the 15 children, by comparison, one-third (five subjects) showed no valid inference at all during the entire phase 1 period; one child, in sharp contrast, showed consistent valid inference (with no invalid inference) throughout phase 1. Of the 10 subjects who showed some valid inference, six showed only a single valid inference on one occasion in one domain during phase 1. Of the remaining four, one, as noted, showed perfect validity (and therefore no improvement), leaving only three subjects contributing to any degree to the statistically significant improvement in validity over time. These three subjects showed negligible valid inference in segment 1 and increasing amounts in segments 2 and 3.

*Phase 2*

Do children maintain their progress, as adults do, when new content is introduced during phase 2? Group data for the six segments of both phases are presented in Figure 5 (which is parallel to Fig. 2 for adults) for the 14 children who completed both phases. None of the three specific contrasts—between segments 3 and 4, segments 3 and 6, and segments 1 and 4—was significant. The overall effect of time, however, did reach significance ($F[5, 65] = 3.80, p < .01$), as did the effect of domain ($F[1, 13] = 9.65, p < .01$), with performance superior in the physical domain.

As noted with respect to phase 1, however, only a few children show inferential improvement. In assessing the question of transfer of inference strategies to new content, it is therefore essential to look at individual patterns. During phase 2, three of the 14 subjects showed no valid inference (two of whom had shown no valid inference during phase 1 and one who had shown a single valid inference). Another three showed only a single valid inference on one occasion in one domain during phase 2. Another three subjects showed only the very slight progress to two valid inferences during all of phase 2 (from zero or one during phase 1). These subjects are thus making valid inferences at such a low rate that it is not meaningful to ask whether the rate is affected by a switch to new problem content.

The remaining five subjects, then, are the ones for whom it is most meaningful to ask how performance changed from segment 3 to segment 4 (when new content was introduced). The subject who showed perfect validity of inferences during phase 1 (Arnie) was not affected by the new problem content and maintained this level of performance throughout phase 2. (All names in this and subsequent chapters are pseudonyms.) Another subject (Danny) showed no valid inference until the middle segment of phase 1, when he began to show some valid inferences in the physical domain; by the final segment of phase 1, his rate of valid inference in the physical domain was .17. During segment 4, when new content was introduced, this rate increased slightly, to .20, and then continued to increase during segments 5 and 6. This progress was not matched, however, in the social domain, where overall validity remained low.

Of the remaining three subjects (Katy, Norman, and Pedro), two showed only a single valid inference during phase 1 and did not begin to show progress until phase 2, one of them during the initial segment (segment 4) and the other not until the middle segment (segment 5). For these subjects, then, exercise of strategies appeared to have provided a foundation for eventual improvement in these strategies, albeit with new content. Only one subject (Pedro) showed any evidence of having been hampered by new content. This subject showed the highest proportion of valid inference of all children except Arnie, although his proportion of valid inference remained below 50% and he showed only modest improvement from phase 1 to phase 2. During phase 2 in both domains, he showed an identical pattern—very few valid inferences until the middle segment and then more during the final segment. This pattern, however, was also identical to the one he showed in phase 1, again in both domains. For this subject, then, getting acquainted with the content of a problem appeared temporarily to constrain the level of strategies applied to it.

## THE NATURE AND USE OF INFERENCE STRATEGIES

### *Quantity and Validity of Inclusion and Exclusion Inferences*

The patterns of usage of individual types of valid and invalid inference by children generally follow those of adults, with a few important exceptions. The frequency data are less complex for children because children did not show the pattern reported for adults of more inferences in the social domain, particularly in phase 1. Children made only slightly fewer inferences overall than adults—an average of 26.37 per problem, roughly equivalent across phases and domains (for comparative adult data, see Fig. 3). Like adults, however, children made many more inferences of inclusion than exclusion ($F[1, 13] = 28.83, p < .001$). The mean was 21.55 inferences for inclusion and 4.82 for exclusion, children thus making even fewer exclusion inferences than adults did, across both phases.

Like adults, children showed lower rates of validity for inclusion than for exclusion. Because of the lower overall validity rates, however, these differences were not as marked in children as they were in adults. During phase 1, rates were .18 and .23 in the physical and .10 and .21 in the social domain for inclusion and exclusion, respectively. During phase 2, they were .22 and .42 in the physical and .11 and .34 in the social domain, respectively. In summary, like adults, children consistently made more inferences of inclusion than exclusion, but inclusion inferences were less likely to be valid.

### *False Inclusion*

Recall that, by phase 2, the inclusion inferences of adults had become almost entirely focused on the evidence (97% of phase 2 false inclusion inferences were evidence based, compared to 90% for phase 1), even though adults continued to interpret the evidence invalidly with a high degree of frequency. Children, in contrast, show a quite different pattern. During phase 1, 43% of children's false inclusion inferences in the physical domain were invalid because they made no reference to the evidence, that is, were entirely theory based. During phase 2, this percentage dropped to 38%. In the social domain, corresponding percentages were 67% and 71% for phases 1 and 2, respectively. Thus, children remain less likely than adults to attend to the evidence, especially in the social domain, and they show little improvement in this respect over time.

Can the earlier reported low frequencies of children's use of multiple-instance evidence be accounted for by their failure to attend to evidence at all? The answer to this question is no. Even if we consider only evidence-based inferences, children's use of single-instance evidence remains high. During phase 1, 43% of children's evidence-based false inclusion inferences in the physical domain made reference to only a single instance. During phase 2, this percentage dropped to 33%. In the social domain, the corresponding percentages were 70% and 71% for phases 1 and 2, respectively. Thus, even when children did attend to the evidence in making inclusion inferences, these were more likely to be based on a single instance than was the case for adults, who rarely made single-instance inferences by phase 2.

Children made generalized inclusion inferences, however, with a frequency very close to that of adults'—7% in the physical domain and 6% in the social. Frequencies of subtypes of generalized inclusion inferences also were similar to those for adults. Correct conclusions, that is, true characterizations of the causal structure, were involved in the case of 64% of generalized inclusion inferences in the physical domain and 42% in the social. The remaining incorrect conclusions were incorrect either because the database of instances generated by the subject was not representative of the true population of instances (8% of all generalized inclusion inferences in the physical domain and 11% in the social) or because the subject incorrectly represented the database that had been generated (28% of all generalized inclusion inferences in the physical domain and 47% in the social). As these percentages reflect, like adults, children were more likely to misuse generalized inclusion inference to reach incorrect conclusions in the social domain.

### *False Exclusion*

Children also made theory-based exclusion inferences more frequently than adults. Their proportion of false exclusion inferences that were theory based was again higher than that of adults. During phase 1, 38% of children's false exclusion inferences in the physical domain were invalid because they were entirely theory based; during phase 2 this percentage dropped only slightly, to 35%. In the social domain, the corresponding percentages were 52% and 57% for phases 1 and 2, respectively (percentages in both domains slightly lower than for theory-based false inclusion inferences). As was the case for adults, children's generalized exclusion inferences were very rare—a total of five were observed, three of them correct. The types of errors observed among the children's false exclusion inferences that were evidence based closely resembled those observed among adults.

### *Valid Inclusion and Exclusion*

Although occurring relatively more rarely than those of adults, children's valid inferences, like adults', included both inclusion and exclusion. Of the five subjects who showed valid inferences with any frequency (more than once or twice during each phase), four developed facility in both inclusion and exclusion, while the achievement of one subject (Norman) was limited to exclusion.

Although children made fewer valid inferences of inclusion or exclusion than adults, their performance equaled that of adults in the respect that the controlled comparisons (necessary for valid inference) that children made were largely intentional—84% overall, very similar to the proportion for adults. In these cases, the subject stated an intent to investigate the effect of the manipulated feature and only that feature; the comparison was not made post hoc after the data were observed. (As noted regarding the findings for adults, however, we cannot be entirely sure that the control aspect of the comparison—holding all other features constant—was intended rather than accidental.)

No children, however, successfully demonstrated presence or absence of an interaction. (As seen in Table 7, one child exhibited a correct interactive final theory, but the full set of four instances necessary to demonstrate it had not been generated.) Nor did children qualify their inferences (i.e., by limiting them to a particular level of another feature) as adults sometimes did. Less than 1% of children's inferences overall included any qualification.

### *Patterns of Change for Individual Inference Types*

Statistical analyses of validity rates over time were not carried out for inclusion and exclusion individually because of the small numbers of valid inferences involved. It is informative, however, to examine these trends with respect to absolute numbers. As was the case for adults, in the case of exclusion, trends of both types—decline in the number of false exclusion and increase in the number of valid exclusion inferences—contributed about equally to overall improvement in validity. In the case of inclusion, however, we see neither of the trends exhibited by adults—a slight increase in valid inferences and a substantial decrease in invalid inferences. The absolute number of valid inclusion inferences showed no increase over time, and the number of invalid inclusion inferences decreased only slightly—a mean decrease of 1.16 inferences from phase 1 to phase 2 in the physical domain and .16 inferences in the social domain. Most of the progress in inferential validity made by children, then, is focused on exclusion; in particular, we do not see the substantial decline in false inclusion inferences over time that was characteristic of adults.

### *The Influence of Theory on Investigation and Inference*

As we have seen, children relied on their theories rather than the evidence to justify their conclusions to a greater extent than did adults. When children did consider the evidence, the influence of theories was still apparent, as was the case for adults. Like adults, children paid more attention to features that they believed to be causal than those they believed noncausal. This difference was reflected both in the number of times a feature was mentioned in statements of intention and the number of times an inference was actually made regarding that feature. In the case of intentions, the theory effect was significant ($F[1, 13] = 10.02, p < .01$). The effect of theory on inferences was also significant ($F[1, 13] = 20.14, p < .001$). In contrast to the case for adults, the effect of theory on validity of inferences does not reach significance for children, most likely because of the low proportion of valid inferences overall among the children.

## AGE GROUP DIFFERENCES IN SUMMARY

The preceding group analyses help identify strategic weaknesses in children's performance that could account for their lesser knowledge acquisition, relative to that of adults. As we have seen, such weaknesses are not of an across-the-board variety. In a number of respects, the investigative strategies of children are equivalent to those of adults. Children confront the task as willingly as adults, making almost as many total inferences (although these are even more focused on inclusion than was the case for adults), and they show a facility comparable to that of adults in investigating the problem space, focusing investigative intent, and coordinating intent and inference (but not in use of multiple-instance evidence).

Where we see the most pronounced difference between children and adults is in children's use of theory-based reasoning to justify their inferences and, as a consequence, in the validity of these inferences. Adults, we saw, soon begin to attend to the evidence, although they may continue to make inferential errors in interpreting it, owing at least in part to the continuing influence of their theories. Children, in contrast, may continue for a prolonged time to examine evidence and yet justify their conclusions on the basis of their theories, especially in the social domain.

Even when they do base their inferences on evidence, however, children's inference strategies remain inferior to those of adults. Children's strategies, we saw, are less likely to meet the criterion for valid inference of being based on a comparison of two or more instances. (Even if we restrict the comparison to multiple-instance inferences, children's validity rates fall below those of adults.) Children's inferential (as opposed to investigative) strategies, then, do not equal those of adults, even though the majority of children display at least some competence in valid inference, even if only a single valid inference on one or two occasions. Finally, like that of adults, children's performance is inferior in the social domain in the numerous cases in which a domain difference appears. We turn now to qualitative data that will shed light on all these characteristics of children's and adults' performance.

# VII. THE PROCESS OF CHANGE

The group data presented in the preceding chapters make clear a number of characteristics of subjects' strategies. A basic and theoretically significant characteristic is variable usage of valid and invalid strategies over a prolonged period of time. Theory-motivated processing may contribute to this variability by disposing subjects toward one inferential strategy on one occasion and toward a different strategy on another. While suggestive, the group data reveal little about the patterns of strategy usage of individual subjects. Although we reported that virtually all subjects showed mixed strategy usage, group data provide no indication of the extent or form of within-subject variability or of the conditions that dispose a subject to apply one strategy as opposed to another in a particular context. Nor do the group data afford much indication of why strategies change in the course of repeated engagement. What are the obstacles to and the facilitators of strategic change? To address these questions, we turn to individual case study data.

Each subject's record across the ten sessions was treated as an individual case study and examined with respect to patterns of knowledge acquisition, strategy usage, and strategy change. Case studies were then compared and examined as a whole to discern common patterns. In this chapter, we present case study material that illustrates such patterns. We draw these examples largely from the social domain, which subjects overall found the more challenging, and we begin with the more fundamental problems encountered by many of the subjects in the younger age group.

## CONFRONTING THE EVIDENCE

Maria is a subject typical of many of our child subjects in the respect that for a long time she did not involve the evidence at all in her reasoning. In the social domain, Maria worked first on the school problem and then in phase 2 switched to the TV problem. Her initial theories in the school problem were causal for three features (teacher's assistant, class size, and noise) and noncausal for the two remaining features. A summary of the problem structure and the evidence that Maria generated in the school problem are presented in Tables 10 and 11.

In explaining the causal mechanism underlying her theory regarding noise, Maria said, "If the teachers want to talk and they [the students] don't listen 'cause they're making too much noise, they won't learn anything." The first instance of evidence that Maria generated was consonant with this theory—a quiet classroom co-occurred with an excellent outcome. With just this single instance of evidence in front of her, Maria did not hesitate to draw conclusions. She attributed the excellent outcome to the presence of a teacher's assistant and the absence of noise in the classroom. Maria offered this justification of her inference regarding the noise feature: "It's better being quiet than being noisy because, if the teacher says something, they won't hear and they'll get in trouble. It's better with the quiet." Maria thus reiterated her theory in interpreting this outcome. Since her justification was entirely theory based, the interviewer introduced the evidence-focus probe ("Does any of the information from the records here in the file cabinet tell you about whether it makes a difference?"), in response to which Maria replied simply, "No."

The second instance that Maria generated involved a noisy classroom and a fair outcome (Table 11), further corroborating her theory. These first two instances are also consistent with Maria's theory regarding class size since the small class is associated with a better outcome than the large

TABLE 10

True Effects for the Two Social Problems

A. School Problem

| | |
|---|---|
| Teacher's assistant (A or −) | Simple causal effect |
| Teacher's recess activity (lounge [G] or playground [P]) | Interactive causal effect (causal only in absence of A) |
| Class size (S, M, L) | Curvilinear causal effect (S > M = L) |
| Sex of principal (m or f) | Noncausal |
| Noise (n or q) | Noncausal |

B. TV Problem

| | |
|---|---|
| Music (M or -) | Simple causal effect |
| Commercials (C or -) | Interactive causal effect (causal only in absence of music) |
| Length (0,[a] 1, 2) | Curvilinear causal effect (0 > 1 = 2) |
| Day (t or w) | Noncausal |
| Humor (f or s) | Noncausal |

[a] 0 = half-hour length.

TABLE 11

EVIDENCE GENERATED BY MARIA FOR THE SCHOOL PROBLEM (PHASE 1)

| | | | | | |
|---|---|---|---|---|---|
| Session 1: | | | Session 4: | | |
| Instance 1 ..... | APSmq | Excl | Instance 13 ..... | APLmq | Good |
| Instance 2 ..... | -GLfn | Fair | Instance 14 ..... | -GSfn | Good |
| Session 2: | | | Instance 15 ..... | -PSmn | Fair |
| Instance 3 ..... | -PLmq | Poor | Instance 16 ..... | AGMfq | Good |
| Instance 4 ..... | AGSfn | Excl | Instance 17 ..... | -GLmq | Fair |
| Instance 5 ..... | -GLmq | Fair | Session 5: | | |
| Instance 6 ..... | AGSmn | Excl | Instance 18 ..... | -PLfn | Poor |
| Instance 7 ..... | -PMfq | Poor | Instance 19 ..... | AGMmq | Good |
| Session 3: | | | Instance 20 ..... | APSmn | Excl |
| Instance 8 ..... | AGLfq | Good | Instance 21 ..... | -GSfq | Good |
| Instance 9 ..... | -PSmn | Fair | Instance 22 ..... | APLmn | Good |
| Instance 10 ..... | -PLmq | Poor | | | |
| Instance 11 ..... | APSfn | Excl | | | |
| Instance 12 ..... | AGLmq | Good | | | |

one. Maria incorporated both these features in her interpretation following the second instance:

> I think that a student will be better maybe with this one [the first instance]. *Why?* Because let's say that this one [instance 2] has 30 kids and this one [instance 1] only has 20. I think this one [instance 1] will be better because, even though it's [still] going to be noisy, it's going to be better because you could listen more without so much noise in the classroom. With more kids, there's more noise. *Does any of the information from the records here in the file cabinet tell you about whether these things make a difference?* No.

In other words, the classroom with fewer children is also quiet and yields an excellent outcome (Table 11), while the class with many children is noisy and yields a fair outcome. Maria makes use of this opportunity to justify her theories regarding both features (noise and size), even though she makes no explicit reference to the evidence and denies that it had any influence on her assertions. Note that Maria has constructed the two initial instances that she examines in such a way that the three remaining features also covary with outcome. Yet she interprets none of these other features as causal. She claimed, for example, that the teacher's activity during recess (playground vs. lounge) made no difference, offering a theory-based justification consonant with her initial theory regarding this feature: "The kids are going to be playing in the yard or eating. The teachers are going to be eating too, so it doesn't make a difference where they are."

The next data that Maria generates, however, complicate matters. Instances 3 and 4 (Table 11) yield an opposite picture with respect to the noise feature—a quiet classroom now co-occurs with a poor outcome and a noisy classroom with an excellent one. How does Maria respond to this theory-discrepant data? In interpreting instance 3, she dealt with the discrepancy by ignoring the noise feature and turning her attention to other features to interpret the outcome. In interpreting instance 4, however, she returned to the noise feature, appearing at first to be influenced by the evidence to make an exclusion judgment, which she quickly qualified: "I found out that it doesn't matter how the classroom is—like, it doesn't matter if it's noisy. Well, it does matter a little bit if it's noisy. *How do you know?* They can't listen very much to the teacher. *Does any of the information from the records here in the file cabinet tell you about whether it makes a difference?* No."

Instances 5 and 6 similarly produce outcomes that are discrepant with Maria's theory about the noise feature (Table 11). Her reaction to instance 5 is initially disorganized, but she then returns to her earlier theory-based mode with no acknowledgment that the evidence shows a conflicting pattern:

> I found out that . . . [pause] . . . I don't know. *Which things did you find out about?* In the quiet . . . [pause] . . . I was going to find out about this one [noise vs. quiet]. *Did you find out about it?* Yeah. *What did you find out?* I think it's better for a class to be quiet than noisy. *How do you know?* Because if they make noise—let's say a guest comes—and they make noise, they won't listen to the guest. *Does any of the information from the records tell you about whether it makes a difference?* No.

Here we see what appears to be Maria's reluctance to undertake any interpretation of theory-discrepant evidence without a substitute theory in place to make sense of it. Her initial uncertainty suggests that she has engaged in some processing of the evidence, but she does not bring the evidence into her justification and denies its relevance when specifically asked. By the fifth instance in the boat problem (which she is working on in parallel with the school problem), by contrast, Maria was already making multiple-instance (but uncontrolled) evidence-based inferences for two features for which theory and evidence were compatible.

In interpreting instance 6 in the school problem, Maria took the easier route of ignoring the noise feature entirely, turning her attention to another feature to explain the outcome. She did not return to the noise feature until instance 10, when her earlier approach reappears: "I found out that, if it's quiet, it's better. *How do you know?* If you remain noisy, it's going to be impossible for the teacher to teach you. *Does any of the information from the records tell you about whether it makes a difference?* No. I'm just saying that because I know." Here, Maria appears to be aware of the source of her assertion and perhaps even that the present evidence does not support it.

The next occasion at which she addresses the noise feature (instance 16), however, provides a very different portrayal of her differentiation between theory and evidence: "I found out that I think that the quiet classroom is better. *How do you know?* Because with noisy, you can't learn anything, and quiet, you could. *How do you know?* Because we tried other ones, and they were noisy and got poor." This is Maria's first evidence-based justification in her work on the school problem, and she clearly maintains that not just this instance but the evidence as a whole supports her belief about the effect of the noise feature—a generalized inclusion inference (see Chap. I). To make this claim, however, she must seriously distort (or invent) evidence: in the database generated to that point, the three instances yielding outcomes of poor all involved quiet, not noisy, classrooms.

In the remainder of her work on the school problem, Maria began to reference the evidence fairly consistently in justifying her claims and to maintain that this evidence supported the theories she espoused, so long as theories and evidence were compatible. When they were not, however, she either ignored the evidence, mischaracterized it, or drew on it selectively. In the case of the noise feature, instance 18 (Table 11) provided a prime opportunity for the latter since a noisy classroom co-occurred with a poor outcome. In constructing instance 18, prior to observing its outcome, Maria's intention had been to investigate the teacher's-assistant feature; the theory-consonant outcome, however, most likely diverted her attention to the noise feature, and she interpreted the outcome in this way: "Maybe because the class was noisy. *How do you know?* Because I have done other records, and they had done excellent when they were quiet." (Of the four excellent outcomes that had occurred to that point, only one had involved a quiet classroom.)

The next instance (19) paired a quiet classroom with a good outcome. In interpreting it, Maria exhibited her frequent tendency to go back to a previous instance for justification (in response to the evidence-focus probe):

> Maybe because the class was quiet. *How do you know?* Because they could learn more. Maybe let's say the teacher's trying to say something very important, and, if they don't hear, they're not going to learn anything. *Does any of the information from the records tell you about whether noise makes a difference?* Yeah, because we had noisy, and it became poor [instance 18], and I think that's bad because if it was noisy they couldn't listen.

Especially noteworthy in this last justification is the conjunctive use of evidence ("we had noisy and it became poor"--a single-instance *co-occurrence* inference) and theory ("I think that's bad because if it was noisy they couldn't listen") to justify the claim.

The final instance (22) poses a greater interpretive challenge since a noisy classroom co-occurs with a good outcome. Maria nonetheless invokes the noise feature to explain the outcome, perhaps because by now she is quite committed to her theory:

> That maybe the quiet is better. *How do you know?* Because if it weren't quiet every kid won't know anything. *Does any of the information from the records tell you about whether noise makes a difference?* I think it's better for people being quiet because they could learn. *Does any of the information from the records tell you about whether noise makes a difference?* Yeah, once I did one of these, and it was quiet, and he got good.

In the final theory assessment for the school problem, Maria maintained that she had found out "for sure" that noise makes a difference and that quiet classrooms were better "because all the ones we had done with quiet had excellent, good, or fair." She omitted any characterization of outcomes for noisy cases.

Maria fared no better in interpreting evidence regarding the other feature that was theory discrepant in her case, teacher's recess activity, which she believed to be noncausal. Although she did make several inferences regarding this feature, they were always theory-based exclusions, and she never recognized this feature's causal power. For features where the initial theory was correct, in contrast, the conclusion remained correct at the final assessment, and gradually, in interpreting the later instances, Maria called on largely single-instance evidence, as well as theory, to justify these conclusions. Her interpretation following instance 13, for example, referred to her causal theory regarding the teacher's-assistant feature but also made reference to the theory-consistent evidence provided by instance 13: "I think the teacher assistant is better than one teacher. *How do you know?* Because I think it's better because the kids can learn more. *Does any of the information from the records tell you about whether it makes a difference?* Yes. *Can you explain?* Because some kids got 'good,' and they had a teacher assistant."

Maria's approach, in sum, initially was to ignore the evidence entirely, maintaining (in response to probing) that it had played no role in her thinking. If prompted, Maria was able to reference the evidence, but she did no more than selectively interpret a fragment of it or, if she did refer to the larger body of evidence, offer a distorted characterization of it. In phase 1 in the social domain, Maria never progressed from single-instance inferences to two-instance (uncontrolled) comparisons, as she did in the physical domain. In the case of the noise feature, she would have found this especially hard to do since as many comparisons contradicted her claim as supported it.

In phase 2, when the TV problem was introduced, these same limitations are in evidence. However, we see gradually increasing reference to the data being generated, especially when they are congruent with theory. These evidence-based inferences remain invalid but involve exclusion as well as inclusion. For example, Maria initially theorized that day of the week was noncausal, and, in interpreting the initial instance generated in this problem (see Tables 10 and 12), she claimed, "I think it doesn't matter if it's Tuesday or Wednesday. *How do you know?* Because kids watch the show every single day, and I don't think the popularity matters which day it is. *Does any of the information from the records here in the file cabinet tell you about whether it makes a difference?* Yes. *Tell me about that.* Because of she or he got 'good.'"

Thus, when prompted to reference the evidence, Maria acknowledged its relevance to her conclusions (which in the school problem she had often denied) as well as its compatibility with her theory. By the time 16 instances had been generated (see Table 12), Maria had progressed to comparative (two-instance) evidence-based inferences regarding this feature: "I found out that I don't think the day of the week matters to a show. I don't think it makes the show popular or not. *How do you know?* Because we have tried one with Wednesday before [instance 15], and I don't think day of the week matters. It was good. And now it's Tuesday, and it's [also] good." Since the instances that Maria compared here vary with respect to commercials and length as well as day, the inference is not a valid one. Yet this inference marks the first time in the social domain that Maria compared two specific, identifiable (rather than invented) instances—an essential foundation for valid inference.

When evidence is theory discrepant, in contrast, Maria's progress is more limited. In the TV problem, the first evidence-based inference (instance 9) that she made for length (a feature she believed noncausal), for

TABLE 12

EVIDENCE GENERATED BY MARIA FOR THE TV PROBLEM (PHASE 2)

| | | | | | |
|---|---|---|---|---|---|
| Session 1: | | | Session 4: | | |
| Instance 1 ..... | M-2ws | Good | Instance 13 ..... | --0tf | Fair |
| Instance 2 ..... | -C0tf | Good | Instance 14 ..... | M-2ws | Good |
| Session 2: | | | Instance 15 ..... | MC1wf | Good |
| Instance 3 ..... | M-0tf | Excl | Instance 16 ..... | M-2tf | Good |
| Instance 4 ..... | -C1ts | Fair | Instance 17 ..... | --0ts | Fair |
| Instance 5 ..... | MC2ws | Good | Session 5: | | |
| Instance 6 ..... | M-0tf | Excl | Instance 18 ..... | M-2wf | Good |
| Instance 7 ..... | --1wf | Poor | Instance 19 ..... | --1ts | Poor |
| Session 3: | | | Instance 20 ..... | MC0wf | Excl |
| Instance 8 ..... | MC0ts | Excl | Instance 21 ..... | M-1wf | Good |
| Instance 9 ..... | --1ws | Poor | Instance 22 ..... | -C1wf | Fair |
| Instance 10 ..... | M-2wf | Good | | | |
| Instance 11 ..... | --2tf | Poor | | | |
| Instance 12 ..... | M-0wf | Excl | | | |

example, involved data conjoined with theory: "We did before 2 hours, half an hour, and 1 hour, and I don't think that makes a difference because people still see their show." By instance 20, no further progress had been made in Maria's reasoning about the length feature, and she never recognized its causal role:

> I think it doesn't matter what the hour is. *How do you know?* Because people and children watch all kinds of shows and all kinds of hours and times. *Does any of the information from the records here tell you about whether it makes a difference?* Yes. Because we did another one, and it was 2 hours, and it came out excellent, and the other one came out bad. *Which one was that?* The other time, last time, we did one, and it was with the other one, and the first one we did was excellent, and the other one was bad.

In other words, (invented) data involving a constant antecedent (2-hour length) that produces variable outcomes provide Maria's justification for (false) exclusion of the length feature.

The humor feature also involved theory-discrepant evidence in Maria's case, and Maria struggled to reconcile her theory that humor was causal with the accumulating discrepant evidence. After initial theory-based reasoning, she made her first evidence-based inference regarding humor during session 3, in response to the theory-discrepant instance (instance 8) of a serious show with an excellent outcome, an outcome that conflicted with her prediction of fair. Maria attempted a reconciliation by particularizing her theory in a way that accommodated the evidence yet protected the theory: "I guess some kids like it serious. *How do you know?* Because I know that some kids like happy and some kids like funny and some kids like serious. *Does any of the information from the records here tell you about whether humor makes a difference?* No." Although Maria denies being influenced by the evidence, her effort to accommodate the instance that she has just generated, and even to make some theoretical sense of it, seems clear.

In interpreting instance 9, Maria's attention was diverted to the length feature. During the remainder of session 3, however, Maria twice more returned to humor (following instances 10 and 12), in each case making a theory-based inference alleging humor to be causal, with no qualification, in response to instances in which the presence of humor is paired with a favorable outcome. When presence of humor yielded a poor outcome (instance 11), she ignored the feature.

During the next session (instance 14), in response to a theory-discrepant instance of a serious show with good outcome (again conflicting with her prediction of "fair"), Maria made a single-instance evidence-based response, following which the qualified theory reemerged: "I guess some people like serious. *How do you know?* Because it turned out good. *So does humor make a difference?* Not that I think serious is better than funny. I think some kids like funny and some kids like serious. It's their opinion what they like. *So does humor make a difference in how popular the show is?* I think they're both the same. *Funny and serious?* Yes." Despite the exclusion inference made at this point, it does not mark a final reconciliation between theory and evidence. Maria subsequently made another exclusion inference for humor, this one based on a comparison of two specific instances (16 and 17): "This one [instance 17] turned out fair [in comparison to an outcome of good for instance 16], so funny and serious were pretty much the same."

In her next involvement with the humor feature (instance 19), however, in response to the theory-consonant outcome of a serious show with a poor outcome, she made a theory-based *inclusion* inference, claiming a positive effect for humor. Yet the final inference regarding humor (instance 21) reflects the new, qualified theory rather than simple inclusion:

> The funny is better than the serious for some kids. *What do you mean by that?* I mean that some kids like serious but most of the kids like funny. *So does whether it's serious or funny make a difference?* I think they're the same because the kids watch shows; one watches serious, and one watches happy, so I don't think it matters. *How do you know?* I knew that already. *Does any of the information from the records here tell you about whether humor makes a difference?* No.

Even though "most of the kids like funny," the theory has evolved into one of exclusion, which is maintained at the final theory assessment. Yet, in effecting this transition from an initially causal to an ultimately noncausal theory by the time of her final encounter with the TV problem, Maria at the end acknowledged no influence of the evidence that she had examined.

Maria never achieved a valid inference in the social domain, despite the indications of progress that we see in her attention to the evidence. Particularly notable is her interpretive effort with respect to the humor variable. Instead of distorting or inventing evidence (as she did earlier for noise in the school problem and to a lesser extent for length in the TV problem), she makes a concerted (even if largely unacknowledged) effort to interpret the evidence and to reconcile it with her theory. Compared to Maria, adult subjects more consistently attended to and acknowledged the relevance of the evidence. It does not follow, however, that the challenges of coordinating theory and evidence disappear, and later in this chapter we return to these challenges as revealed in the case studies of adults.

In both the physical and the social domains, Maria showed very limited achievement with respect to validity of inferences (one valid inference is made during phase 1 and one during phase 2, both in the physical domain).

Consistent with the greater proportion of evidence-based reasoning in the physical domain characteristic of the sample as a whole, however, Maria's inferences in the physical domain were more likely to be evidence based and more likely to be multiple than single instance. Evidence-based two-instance false inclusion inferences were in fact the modal type that she displayed for both problems in the physical domain. In contrast to Maria, some other children did progress to significant use of valid inference, as we examine in the next section.

## THE EMERGENCE OF VALID STRATEGIES

As reflected in the group data, only a few children progressed any further than Maria's achievement of evidence-based comparisons of two uncontrolled instances. One such subject (Arnie), recall, showed valid inference throughout (a performance that exceeded that of any of the adults). Most informative, however, are the children who showed a transition from an absence of valid inference to valid inference of some frequency. Close observation of these subjects' progress offers the greatest opportunity of gaining insight into how and why new strategies emerge when they are initially absent. (The adult sample provides a lesser opportunity in this respect since the majority of adults, recall, showed some valid inference at the initial session.)

Of the four children who exhibit this transition, two show no progress until phase 2. In the case of Norman, progress did not appear until session 4 of phase 2 (the ninth of the 10 sessions). Prior to this time, he had shown only a single valid inference (at session 4 of phase 1 in the physical domain)—a valid two-instance inclusion inference in which no other features were varied and the inference was compatible with his theory. During the first three sessions of phase 2, Norman's modal inference type was two-instance false inclusion in the physical domain and single-instance false inclusion in the social domain, always compatible with his theoretical beliefs. There was no false exclusion, and features believed noncausal were not examined.

Then, in the middle of session 4 (phase 2) in the physical domain, working with the car problem, Norman made a successful prediction on the basis of two features he (correctly) believed causal, but, on seeing the outcome, he expressed his dissatisfaction: "*What did you find out?* I didn't find out nothing. I found this out last time. I found out everything last time. But, no, wait, I got to try one more thing else. I want to do an experiment. In the colors. I want to see if the colors really do make a difference or not." Norman then generated two successive instances varying only with respect to color and concluded that color made no difference. He produced a similar two-instance comparison for color again in this same session; these marked the only attention he had paid to the color feature (which he had theorized to be noncausal).

In the social domain, it is similarly at session 4 of phase 2 (which took place a few days after session 4 in the physical domain) that valid exclusion first appears. In this case, however, theoretical belief had wavered between causal and noncausal, and the immediately preceding inference had involved false inclusion of this feature (sex of principal in the TV problem): "I think it turned out pretty good. *Why?* Because it has a man principal. I think a man principal is better than a woman principal. *How do you know?* I don't know that. It's just a lucky guess. I think that, but I'm not sure. *What would you have to do to be sure?* I would have to try it again. *And how do you know now that a man principal is better?* Because, you see, it came out good because they have a man principal. But I'm not so sure."

Norman was then invited to generate another instance, and he said, "I'm going to find out if the man principal or the woman principal is better." He chose an instance that varied from the previous one only with respect to this feature, and, on observing the outcome, he concluded, "I think I know what's wrong now. I don't think it matters if it's a woman or a man. *How do you know?* I do it the same way, and it comes out good. I put it different, and it comes out good. I put a man principal, it comes out good. I put a woman principal, it comes out good. So that's not our main problem." Norman's inferential success was limited to exclusion (except for the single valid inclusion inference in phase 1), but this valid exclusion strategy appeared at a distinct point in his endeavors across the two domains, and he appeared to gain some awareness of its power ("I do it the same way, and it comes out good"), a power that enables him to definitively exclude the feature ("So that's not our main problem").

In addition to the issue of cross-domain synchrony in the emergence of new strategies, Norman's case study raises the general question of whether emergence of a new strategy is more likely to occur when theory and evidence are compatible or when the subject is trying to interpret discrepant evidence. Case studies of the three other subjects whom we consider here, like the one of Norman, indicate that both possibilities occur.

Danny first showed valid inclusion in session 3 (phase 1) in the social domain and in session 4 (phase 1) in the physical domain. In the social domain, the inference was made in a context of theory-evidence compatibility; in the physical domain, theory and evidence were discrepant. Danny first showed valid exclusion in session 5 in both domains, and in both cases theory and evidence were discrepant. (As noted in Chap. VI, however, Danny's valid inference was not maintained in the social domain during phase 2.) Similarly, in the case of Pedro, both valid inclusion and valid exclusion emerged during session 2 of phase 1 in the physical domain and during the second (inclusion) and third (exclusion) sessions of phase 1 in the social domain; in three of the four cases, the context was theory compatible; in one, it was theory discrepant.

The final subject, Katy, first showed valid inclusion in session 2 of phase 1 in both domains; in the physical domain theory and evidence were compatible, and in the social domain they were discrepant. The emergence of valid exclusion in Katy's record was the only instance reflecting any significant asynchrony across domains. Valid exclusion emerged in session 3 of phase 1 in the social domain but not until session 2 of phase 2 in the physical domain (in both cases in a theory-discrepant context).

These case study data do not tell us why new strategies emerge precisely when they do. They do, however, illustrate kinds of data that can illuminate the process of developmental change and answer certain questions about its features. We have more to say in this respect in the final chapter. Summarizing the findings presented in this section, the evidence for cross-domain emergence of new strategies is positive. Conditions for their emergence, however, appear to be variable. Depending on the outcome of a controlled comparison, the inference may be one of inclusion or exclusion, and the context may be either theory discrepant or theory compatible.

## APPLYING STRATEGIES EFFECTIVELY

We turn now to an equally challenging set of questions raised by the adult data. To a much greater overall extent than children, adult subjects attended to the data, making largely evidence-based inferences comparing at least two instances of evidence. Adult subjects all had strategies of valid inclusion and exclusion in their repertories. Why, then, were they not able to apply these strategies consistently in order to identify with a greater degree of success at least the simple causal and noncausal effects that were operating in each of the problems?

The case study of Geoff, an adult subject who worked first on the TV problem in the social domain, affords some insight into the most fundamental of the problems that subjects confronted. When Geoff was asked to choose his first record, he said he was going to "pick just any program." The record he chose to see was of a program with commercials but without music or humor, 2 hours long and on Tuesday, with an outcome of "fair" (see Table 13). Asked what he had found out, Geoff offered this interpretation: "You see, this shows you that the factors I was saying about . . . that you have to be funny to make it good or excellent, and the day doesn't really matter, and it's too long."

Geoff's inference is slightly more complex than many because he is interpreting a negative instance—absence of humor and brevity leads to a

TABLE 13

Evidence Generated by Geoff for the TV Problem (Phase 1, Sessions 1 and 2)

| | | |
|---|---|---|
| Session 1: | | |
| Instance 1 | -C2ts | Fair |
| Instance 2 | MC0wf | Excellent |
| Instance 3 | M-1wf | Good |
| Session 2: | | |
| Instance 4 | MC0wf | Excellent |
| Instance 5 | M-2wf | Good |
| Instance 6 | --2ws | Poor |
| Instance 7 | MC2ts | Good |
| Instance 8 | MC2tf | Good |
| Instance 9 | MC2wf | Good |

poor outcome. Yet his is nonetheless a classic false inclusion inference in which one or more features are causally implicated in an outcome based simply on the co-occurrence of a particular level of the feature and the outcome. In this case, Geoff implicates both humor and length on this basis while excluding day of the week without evidence-based justification. When asked to choose a second record, Geoff added humor and music and changed the length to a half hour and the day to Wednesday (Table 13). The outcome was excellent, and his interpretation was as follows: "It has basically what I thought. It does make a difference when you put music and have commercials and the length of time and the humor. Basically the day is the only thing that doesn't really matter."

We thus see how Geoff utilized the two pieces of evidence that he chose initially as an opportunity to confirm all his initial theories. He interpreted three of the factors that covaried with outcome (music, humor, and length) over the two instances as causal. He also included the commercials factor as causal, despite the fact that it did not vary, while he nonetheless excluded day, which did vary, as noncausal. None of these inferences, of course, is valid. This brief excerpt serves as an illustration of how subjects were able to engage the evidence consistently, drawing on it as a basis for their inferences (in contrast to subjects like Maria, who frequently denied its relevance), without its having any influence on their theories.

Before the end of the second session, Geoff had generated and intended to interpret a potentially valid comparison (instances 7 and 8). In generating instance 8, he predicted, "I know that, if we make it funny, it will be even better." The outcome, however, remained the same (good), providing the opportunity for a valid exclusion strategy. But Geoff shied away from this interpretation and instead concluded, "It [the rating] was less than I expected. This brings me back to what I thought. . . . It's rated less because it's too long." Thus, rather than make a theory-incompatible inference, Geoff shifted the explanatory burden to another feature. We know, furthermore, that Geoff understood and could use the valid exclusion strategy because the very next instance that he generated (instance 9) enabled him to achieve his stated intent of "finding out that the day doesn't make a difference." The outcome was again good, and he concluded, "The day doesn't make a difference because the previous one was a different day and it still was good." Note that the identical evidence led to the application of different strategies and yielded different conclusions in the case of the day-of-week feature than it did in the case of humor.

We see here the difficulty that Geoff has relinquishing a causal theory (a difficulty we also observed in Maria), even though he must compromise the validity and consistency of his inference strategies to save the theory. This challenge was the most difficult one for all our subjects, especially in the social domain. Subjects had much less difficulty detecting covariation where they did not anticipate it and constructing a causal theory to explain it. Indeed, a single feature/outcome co-occurrence may be sufficient to provoke construction of a new causal theory. For example, like most subjects when they worked with the TV problem, Eddie initially believed that day of week was noncausal. After Wednesday had co-occurred first with a good and later with an excellent outcome, however, Eddie invented a theory to make it causal: "[It makes a difference] because suppose these children go to school and on Tuesday they have to sit down and do their homework. On Wednesday they will be relieved. *So they like Wednesday shows better?* Yes, because it is the middle of the week. *Does anything you have found out here tell you that they like Wednesday shows better?* Yes, because this show got an excellent." Once such theories were in place, they tended to be maintained, even in the face of conflicting data and at the cost of the variable criteria for the application of strategies that were seen in Geoff's case.

## DEVICES FOR PROTECTING THEORIES

What was the longer-term outcome of the shifting criteria for strategy application that subjects like Geoff exhibited? The most frequent answer is that such biases were maintained, resulting in a disinclination to apply to certain features the valid strategies that had been practiced and perfected with respect to others. The intent appeared to be one of protecting the theories in which the subject had an investment. We can again consider as an illustration the case of a subject, Carmen, who, like Geoff, was unable to relinquish her theory that humor in the TV problem was causal. Carmen took the first instance that she examined (MC0wf with excellent outcome; see Table 14) as evidence that her theory regarding humor was correct.

The next two instances (Table 14), however, form a controlled compari-

TABLE 14

EVIDENCE GENERATED BY CARMEN FOR THE TV PROBLEM (PHASE 1)

| | | | | | | |
|---|---|---|---|---|---|---|
| Session 1: | | | Session 4: | | |
| Instance 1 ..... | MC0wf | Excl | Instance 15 ..... | MC0wf | Excl |
| Instance 2 ..... | M-1wf | Good | Instance 16 ..... | MC0tf | Excl |
| Instance 3 ..... | M-1ws | Good | Instance 17 ..... | --2ws | Poor |
| Instance 4 ..... | MC2tf | Good | Instance 18 ..... | --2ts | Poor |
| Session 2: | | | Instance 19 ..... | --2tf | Poor |
| Instance 5 ..... | MC0ws | Excl | Session 5: | | |
| Instance 6 ..... | --1ts | Poor | Instance 20 ..... | --2ws | Poor |
| Instance 7 ..... | -C2tf | Fair | Instance 21 ..... | --2ts | Poor |
| Instance 8 ..... | MC0wf | Excl | Instance 22 ..... | -C2ts | Fair |
| Instance 9 ..... | MC1ws | Good | Instance 23 ..... | -C0ts | Good |
| Session 3: | | | Instance 24 ..... | MC2tf | Good |
| Instance 10 ..... | MC0tf | Excl | | | |
| Instance 11 ..... | --2ts | Poor | | | |
| Instance 12 ..... | --1tf | Poor | | | |
| Instance 13 ..... | MC2wf | Good | | | |
| Instance 14 ..... | MC0wf | Excl | | | |

son that would allow her to disconfirm the theory. In choosing instance 3, she said, "Let's take a chance with serious. I don't think they'll rate it very high." When the outcome contradicted this prediction, Carmen first appeared to relinquish her causal theory regarding humor, by means of a valid exclusion strategy: "*What have you found out?* Children are just as interested in watching the serious stuff. They do not necessarily have to watch something with humor." The interviewer went on, however, to inquire: "*So does it make a difference whether there is humor or not?* Yes it does, because in the other one [instance 1] they rated excellent, but here they just rated it good, so humor still overpowers the seriousness. I think children would understand comedy better than if it is serious." Thus, comparing instances 2 and 3, Carmen drew the correct inference, but this conclusion apparently did not sit well with her, and, in response to a further probe, she instead compared instance 3 to instance 1, enabling her to draw a different (and invalid) inference. Furthermore, she justified this inference with theory-based reasoning—this is a conclusion that makes sense, she suggests. In choosing instance 4, Carmen then turned her attention to a different factor entirely.

At session 2, however, Carmen returned to humor. Here (instance 5) the outcome strongly contradicts her humor theory. She again showed a similar sequence of first valid, then invalid reasoning, and we can sense her confusion: "I did not think the children would have gone for it. I was thinking that they might . . . if they had rated poor . . . but I see that it does not, this is a good one." But Carmen then took a different tack: "You see, it's not that serious because it has music in it. Maybe that's what made a difference."

The outcome of the next instance (6) allowed Carmen to pursue this line of thought. The absence of music, she inferred, played a role, but humor also "helped": "If I had put fun in, I think that children would have rated it a little bit better." In choosing the next instance (7), Carmen hoped to improve the outcome (and thereby demonstrate the power of the humor factor): "I hope that humor will play a big part in it." The outcome was only slightly better, however, and she concluded, "Oh, music still plays a big part. . . . The fact there was no music made a difference in how they rated it. *Anything else?* Maybe humor helped."

Still holding onto her humor theory, and having established to her satisfaction that music also plays a causal role, Carmen then turned to the common strategy of trying to maximize the overall outcome: "I'll do what I think is positive now." This strategy, note, sets up the conditions for false inclusion inference. The alleged positive levels of factors believed to be causal are carried along with those that a subject may already have validly established as causal. In other words, the ineffective factor attains its illusory causal power through its deliberate covariation with an actual causal factor.

Carmen exploited this strategy with instance 8, implicating both music and humor, as well as length, as causal. In choosing the final instance (9) at this session, Carmen appeared to turn her attention to length, predicting an outcome of good because the program was longer than the one in instance 8. In interpreting the outcome, however, she initially said nothing about length and instead exploited the opportunity to note the apparent implication regarding humor (which she had also varied): "They seem not to like it serious. When it had humor, they rated it excellent."

At the third session, we see more of the same. Regarding instance 12, Carmen noted, "They rated it bad, even though humor was involved." Rather than relinquish the humor theory, however, a reference to instance 10 allowed her to reach this notable conclusion: "I found out that humor and music together make a difference."

The comparison of instances 13 and 14 produces the first valid inclusion inference, for length, and at session 4 the tide seems to turn, with two successive valid exclusion inferences for day of the week (based on a comparison of instances 15 and 16 and instances 17 and 18). Presumably because it fit well with her theoretical beliefs, Carmen liked to demonstrate the irrelevance of this feature and did so repeatedly. Then, with instances 18 and 19, Carmen set the stage for a similar valid exclusion of humor. But here, where her theoretical involvement is greater, Carmen instead concluded, with evident disappointment, "I thought humor might balance all these, but it did not. They still rated it bad." In other words, she believed that the presence of humor might compensate for the absence of the other features that she perceived as positive (music and a short length). Instead of using the data that she had generated to make an exclusion inference for humor, however, Carmen drew this conclusion: "I think humor still makes a difference. *How do you know?* From previous ratings. . . . Every time the humor was with the music, they rated it excellent. *And what did you learn from this instance [19] here?* They rated it bad. In this particular one, humor did not make a difference."

Carmen's final session with the TV problem shows clearly sophisticated and efficient strategy use. Instances 20 and 21 were used to validly exclude day. Instance 21 was then used again with instance 22 to validly include commercials and 22 and 23 to validly include length. For humor, however, Carmen does not construct the controlled comparison that she has by now shown herself quite capable of. Instead, in constructing the final instance (24), she changed three variables rather than only one, thereby not risking putting her humor theory to a serious test. In interpreting instance 24, she concluded that humor was causal, with the justification, "When I chose serious, even with commercials, the rating was bad."

Carmen exhibits two means of saving an incorrect theory that were common to many subjects. The first is to particularize an inference—"In this particular one, humor did not make a difference"—with the implication that the theory was by no means dead and might well apply elsewhere. The second, and more common, strategy is to particularize the theory, by linking the factor to another one with perceived causal power—"humor and music together make a difference."

Still another means that subjects used to save a theory, one that we saw in Maria's case, is to invent data to which an inference strategy can be applied, enabling the subject to maintain compatibility between theory and evidence. Invention of data was by no means limited to children. During his second session with the TV problem, an adult subject, Juan, for example, justified his claim that day of the week makes no difference with the assertion that, "I tried it with both days and got the same outcome." In fact, he had generated instances involving both days, but these were uncontrolled with respect to other features, and they never yielded the same outcome. Data invention is particularly likely to arise in the case of generalized inferences, given the freedom in characterizing data that they allow. (Recall that one-quarter to one-third of generalized inferences involved invented data.)

In the cases that we have presented, subjects' investigation is theory driven to a counterproductive extent. A major problem with highly theory-driven investigation is that subjects do not access enough of the database to disconfirm their theories. They are satisfied with the average one-third of the data that they access and are convinced that the information that they have is sufficient to warrant firm conclusions.

Failure to generate sufficient data is by no means the whole problem, however. The excerpts presented from Carmen's protocol suggest that no amount of data would have led her to exclude humor as a factor. More broadly, the limitations in reasoning shown by Geoff and Carmen can be characterized as metastrategic, rather than strategic, in nature. Strategic competence, that is, the ability to execute valid inference strategies, was observed in all the adult subjects. Where subjects appear weak, in contrast, is in reflection on both the valid and the invalid strategies that they use, in a way that might promote their consistent application. As these excerpts illustrate, in the absence of this metastrategic competence, claims can be justified by identifying even the most minimal piece of evidence that appears to support them. And, as we have seen, subjects may apply a variety of devices to protect these claims from the evidence that bears on them. In cases in which the evidence is acknowledged, these devices include particularizing the instance (as an exception) or particularizing the theory (by limiting its applicability). Alternative devices include simply ignoring the evidence and/or inventing different evidence. We return to the topic of metastrategic competence in the final chapter.

## COORDINATING MULTIPLE FEATURES

While metastrategic weaknesses were clearly evident, strategic weaknesses in adult subjects' performance were not absent. Subjects' strategic competence in executing tests for simple effects was not matched by competence in assessing second-order (interactive) effects. Subjects often postulated interactive effects, but they rarely were able to provide the appropriate evidence to substantiate these claims. What are the challenges involved? Our case study data suggest that they parallel the demands entailed in assessing simple effects, but at a more complex, second-order level.

In particular, two different kinds of difficulties were identified. The first is the need to coordinate the multiple comparisons involved in testing for an interaction effect, in a way that maintains a focus on the goal to be achieved. A minimum of four instances must be coordinated—two to establish the presence (or absence) of an effect at one level of another feature and two more to assess whether the presence (or absence) of this effect holds at a different level of the other feature. As subjects undertook this task, they often lost track of what they were doing, and their attention was diverted to another feature than the one they had set out to investigate. This same coordination problem was observed occasionally in the investigation of simple first-order effects—a comparison was constructed to assess the effect of one feature, but the subject's attention became diverted to another feature before an inference regarding the first feature was made. In the case of second-order effects, however, the specific form of the needed comparisons makes the danger of losing focus especially likely.

An example is provided by Flora, who at the beginning of her third session with the TV problem (see Table 15) achieved a valid exclusion of the commercials feature on the basis of a controlled comparison of instances that involved the 2-hour length (instances 11 and 12). She then stated an intent to find out "whether commercials in a shorter length make a difference." To do so, she chose instance 13. Note, however, that comparison of this instance with the preceding one is also a controlled comparison that allows for assessment of the effect of the length feature, and this is exactly where Flora's attention was diverted in making an interpretation following instance 13: "*What have you found out?* The length of the program does not make a difference. *How do you know?* Because I got the same thing with the previous one, and it was 2 hours."

The fourth instance needed to complete the interaction test (between commercials and length) was never constructed. Instead, Flora then went on to make exactly the same mistake in the case of humor. Having earlier made an (invalid) inclusion inference for humor at the 1-hour length, she wanted to explore its effect in the case of shorter (half-hour) programs—"whether humor matters when the program is shorter." Instead of maintaining her focus on humor and constructing the appropriate comparison to fulfill her intention, however, Flora concluded (validly) following instance 15, "The length is an important factor."

A second difficulty that was observed—one that also closely parallels a common difficulty in the investigation of simple effects—involves, at the strategic level, maintaining the necessary control of other variables and, at the metastrategic level, understanding the significance of doing so. In her work on the school problem during phase 2, Flora exhibited this difficulty as well. She had by now overcome the limitations exhibited in the first phase, maintaining her focus on the assessment of second-order rather than simple effects and completing the generation of the requisite four instances to demonstrate an interaction effect.

TABLE 15

EVIDENCE GENERATED BY FLORA FOR THE TV PROBLEM (PHASE 1, SESSION 3)

| Session 3: | | |
|---|---|---|
| Instance 11 ............ | M-2ws | Good |
| Instance 12 ............ | MC2ws | Good |
| Instance 13 ............ | MC1ws | Good |
| Instance 14 ............ | M-1wf | Good |
| Instance 15 ............ | M-0wf | Excl |

At the second session with the school problem (instance 7), Flora stated an intent to further examine the effect of principal's sex, which she had validly excluded at session 1 (instances 1 and 2, Table 16): "Sex of the principal did not make a difference when there was no assistant, quiet, medium, and [teacher in the] lounge. Now I want to see whether it makes a difference here with this class." This time she did bring the test to a conclusion, comparing instances 7 and 8: "Sex of the principal does not make a difference, and it does not change when the class changes."

Although Flora gave some indication that her intent was to focus on class size (small vs. medium) as the feature with which principal's sex might interact, note that she changed all the remaining variables as well (as Flora notes, the instance 1 and 2 comparison at session 1 involved no assistant, quiet, and lounge, while this one, comparing instances 7 and 8, involved teacher's assistant, noise, and playground). As a result, her test is not a valid test of a second-order effect involving principal's sex and class size. If the result of the second comparison had been a difference in outcomes, Flora would not have known which of the remaining features interacted with sex (since she had varied them all). What we have, then, is the replication of a simple effect (or lack of effect) for a different constellation of features, not a test for a second-order effect of two specific features. This need to control the remaining features across the two two-instance comparisons (in order to achieve a valid test of interaction between two features) parallels, of course, the need to control the remaining features *within* a two-instance comparison in assessing simple effects.

In subsequent investigation, Flora moved toward such control, main-

TABLE 16

Evidence Generated by Flora for the School Problem (Phase 2)

| Instance | Features | Outcome |
|---|---|---|
| Session 1: | | |
| Instance 1 ..... | -GMmq | Fair |
| Instance 2 ..... | -GMfq | Fair |
| Instance 3 ..... | AGMfq | Good |
| Instance 4 ..... | APMfq | Good |
| Session 2: | | |
| Instance 5 ..... | APLmq | Good |
| Instance 6 ..... | APSmq | Excl |
| Instance 7 ..... | APSfn | Excl |
| Instance 8 ..... | APSmn | Excl |
| Instance 9 ..... | AGSfn | Excl |
| Session 3: | | |
| Instance 10 ..... | -PMmn | Poor |
| Instance 11 ..... | -PMmq | Poor |
| Instance 12 ..... | -GMmq | Fair |
| Instance 13 ..... | -GMfq | Fair |
| Instance 14 ..... | AGMfq | Good |
| Session 4: | | |
| Instance 15 ..... | AGSfq | Excl |
| Instance 16 ..... | AGLfq | Good |
| Instance 17 ..... | APLfq | Good |
| Instance 18 ..... | APLfn | Good |
| Instance 19 ..... | APSfn | Excl |
| Session 5: | | |
| Instance 20 ..... | AGSfq | Excl |
| Instance 21 ..... | APSfq | Excl |
| Instance 22 ..... | APSfn | Excl |
| Instance 23 ..... | APSmn | Excl |
| Instance 24 ..... | APMmn | Good |

taining it for two of the three remaining features in her next exploration of interaction and finally achieving total control in the investigation of teacher's recess activity (lounge vs. playground), carried out during session 3. She evaluated this feature at both levels of the teacher's-assistant variable, recalling first that the lounge and the playground yielded equivalent outcomes in the presence of a teacher's assistant (instances 3 and 4), then determining that, in the absence of a teacher's assistant, they yield different outcomes (instances 11 and 12). (Variation of principal's sex did not invalidate the comparison since this feature had been validly excluded.)

Despite appropriate execution of the test, however, Flora was not able to draw the appropriate interaction inference. The problem was perhaps that she had not specifically focused on teacher's assistant as the feature whose interaction with recess activity was being assessed. To do so she may have needed a theoretical conceptualization that would have allowed her to make sense of such an interaction. In any case, what she did instead was to regard the second comparison as simply a replication of the first (rather than as a test for the interaction of two particular features). As a result, she was confused by the outcome—the failure to replicate—and could draw no conclusion other than to note her confusion, which is amplified by the fact that both outcomes conflict with her theoretical belief: "The teacher's activity is confusing because first I got that it does not make any difference and then I get that it is better in the lounge, whereas I think that it would have to be better when teachers are in the playground with the kids."

At session 4, Flora returned to this same feature, this time again assessing it in the presence of a teacher's assistant and observing no effect (instances 16 and 17). She first expressed utter confusion but then finally appeared to grasp the interaction: "Do you want me to go crazy? My God! *What did you find out?* First I did an experiment in which I got that it did not make a difference, and now I get a difference, and now again I do this, and it does not make a difference. *So what does it mean?* Just now what was different was that it had a teacher's assistant. So if it has a teacher's assistant, the teacher can be in any place [during recess]. It does not make any difference." The interviewer then asked Flora to justify this conclusion, and Flora went into a long review of all the relevant data. At the end, however, when the interviewer asked her to sum up, she drew this conclusion: "The majority is no difference. I did three, and I got that in two it made no difference. So I go for no difference."

At the final session, Flora again turned her attention to this feature, but this time she simplified matters even further. Instead of maintaining the replication conception reflected in her previous effort, she simply tested the effect of the recess activity feature one time, with teacher's assistant present (instances 20 and 21). She first predicted and then concluded (on the basis of the constant outcome) the absence of an effect—"it does not make a difference"—with no reference to the conflicting findings obtained at earlier sessions.

Although space precludes a detailed characterization, during this same period Flora exhibited parallel difficulty with interaction in the boat problem. She could not reconcile her repeated finding that weight makes a difference in small boats with her finding that it does not in large boats, and she focused much of her investigation (13 of the 24 instances that she generated) on this puzzle. By the end of session 3 with the boat problem, she had progressed no further than to note that, "today, the weight didn't make any difference; last session it did." The final session she devoted entirely to this issue, indicating at the outset that she was going to investigate "the weight in the big boat because this is what keeps me confused," and noted the conflicting influence of her own theory—"I think [weight] does make a difference, but in this boat it does not make a difference." Ultimately, however, she was able to state the interaction ("In the small boat the weight makes a difference, but it does not in the large boat"), an achievement that she never reached in the school problem.

Again, space constraints preclude detailed examination, but it is worth noting that the qualitative data from our case studies show parallel kinds of problems when subjects try to deal with simple additive (rather than interactive) effects. A number of subjects undertook to demonstrate the simultaneous operation of these effects after they had established most of the simple effects to their satisfaction. In their efforts to do so, their previously valid strategies were likely to be compromised. After having exhibited valid inclusion and valid exclusion repeatedly during earlier sessions, Nina, for example, working with the TV problem during phase 1, compared two instances in which length was varied and music was consistently absent (-C0tf and -C1tf), but she was unable to draw the straightforward inference that followed regarding the length feature. "What I'm not sure," she explained, "is was it the length of time that made the difference [to the second instance] or was it the lack of music." Later she elaborated, "I'll know definitely when I add the music."

Nina was clearly thinking here of effects as alternatives and could not conceptualize them as functioning additively. By the end of the second phase, however, working now on the school problem, she had achieved this understanding. She replicated the effect of teacher's assistant at two levels of class size and in addition made the appropriate cross-comparisons among these four instances to establish an effect of class size as well, allowing her to conclude, "The assistant makes a big difference, but so does the size of the class."

Very few subjects achieved this coordination of multiple effects. Yet, in both scientific and everyday contexts, effects occur not in isolation but in conjunction and often interaction with others. The excerpts presented here show the challenge that thinking about such multiple effects poses, even when attention is focused squarely on the data. When Nina asks herself was it this feature or that one that made the difference (rather than conceiving of the possibility that they operate additively), the constraint that she imposes on her own thinking is one that most likely prevails in most everyday reasoning. In the final chapter, we consider further how strategic limitations like those examined here combine and interact with metastrategic limitations to constrain reasoning.

# VIII. CONCLUSIONS

The purpose of the research reported in this *Monograph* has been to examine how strategies of knowledge acquisition operate and how they change developmentally. Knowledge acquisition is an enormously broad construct, and we make no pretense of having addressed the topic in its entirety. Infants and young children begin early in their lives to acquire knowledge of much simpler forms than we have been concerned with here, while older children and adults acquire knowledge of considerably greater complexity than the causal effect of a single factor on another. Nonetheless, understanding the causal effect of one factor on another is a core building block of more complex forms of understanding, and it is here that we have focused our study of the knowledge acquisition process. We do so by asking subjects to acquire knowledge of multivariable causal systems that are simple in structure but nonetheless invoke a rich base of preexisting knowledge that must be integrated with new evidence.

To study processes of knowledge acquisition extended over time, we use a microgenetic method. What has it revealed that more conventional methods would not have? Understanding the change process is the original purpose to which the microgenetic method was addressed. Our study complements earlier work in this respect (see Chap. I), with the added features of the simultaneous examination of two forms of change (in knowledge and strategies) and the comparison of the change process at two different points in the life span. We begin, however, with the implications of our work that address broader issues, even, than the process of developmental change. They center on two broad characteristics of reasoning strategies investigated by means of microgenetic analysis—variability (over repeated occasions) and generality (over a range of content as well as populations).

## BROAD IMPLICATIONS OF MICROGENETIC ANALYSIS

### *Variability*

Our results amply document intraindividual variability in strategy usage, in an adult as well as a child population. Both children and adults possess a range of different strategies and use them selectively and variably across repeated occasions within a constant problem environment. This variability has been observed in earlier microgenetic research with children (see Chap. I). An important inference to be drawn from the present results is that such variability is not unique to children or to periods of developmental transition. Rather, it appears to be a more general characteristic of cognitive functioning, at least for the kinds of cognitive strategies and age groups examined thus far in microgenetic research.

An immediate implication of within-subject variability as a general characteristic of cognitive functioning has to do with assessment. Single-occasion, single-task assessment of cognitive competencies is likely to provide an incomplete, if not misleading, characterization of an individual's ability. A more accurate portrayal would take the form of a frequency distribution across a range of strategies. Even this characterization could well be misleading, however, since a subject's strategy usage, we have seen, is likely to evolve with repeated engagement, typically toward greater reliance on more adequate strategies and reduced reliance on less adequate ones. Such improvement appears not to be unlimited given continued engagement—our adult subjects showed more improvement during the first half of their engagement with the problems than they did during the second half. Rather, performance may show some "leveling off" after an initial period of engagement. Although the particular duration of such a period would be likely to differ for different kinds of tasks, the general implication is that the level of performance toward the end of this period is likely to provide a more informative picture of a subject's competence than would initial performance. This conclusion accords with current literature in the field of adult development based on psychometric task performance (Baltes, 1987).

### *Variability and Cross-Task Generality*

A second, equally broad implication of intraindividual variability appears when assessment is extended across multiple content domains, as it was in the present case. In the typical single-occasion assessment of strategy generality across tasks differing in content but requiring comparable strategies, subjects show some variability in performance across tasks. These differences are typically regarded under the heading of *content effects,* the implication being that differences in particular task content or broader task domains are responsible for the observed variability in performance. In other words, the variability resides in the task.

The present results, however, suggest another conceptualization, one based on a view of the strategies applied to a particular task on a given occasion as simply a sample from a distribution of possible strategies that might have been applied to this task (if the task had remained constant and administration repeated). If a second task differing in content is added and variability in performance is observed across tasks, at least part of this variability may be attributable to variation that resides within the subject (since it could have appeared even if the task had remained constant) rather than only within the task. This is a significantly different conception of content variability (or *décalage* in the Piagetian literature) than the one that has prevailed in most discussions of the topic. The broad implication is that cross-task strategy generality is constrained by within-task within-subject strategic variability.

### *Generality and Transfer*

As the primary means of assessing the generality of strategies, we situated a traditional transfer design within a microgenetic framework. The results were unambiguous. Improvement that took place within a domain generalized to different content when a new problem was substituted within each domain midway through the period of observation. The microgenetic design made it possible to observe this transfer within the context of overall variability in performance.

Our transfer findings fit better into one rather than the other of the two conceptualizations of transfer described in Chapter I. In one, transfer depends on overlap between the representations of two problem domains (see Chap. I). Another conception focuses on the subject's activity, with transfer depending on the extent to which activity is common to two settings (Greeno et al., 1993). Our subjects were engaging in activities that enabled them to acquire knowledge within particular problem domains. The different problems afforded equivalent opportunities for engaging in and developing skill in these activities. The transfer data establish that movement from one problem to another did not interfere with the progress that was occurring.

These positive transfer findings are notable in an atmosphere in which transfer is "on trial" (Detterman & Sternberg, 1993) as notoriously difficult to document and perhaps even nonexistent (Detterman, 1993). Why did our subjects show transfer of newly developing cognitive strategies when transfer so often fails to occur in both children and adults? One explanation may be that our paradigm fulfills the two conditions proposed by Sternberg and Frensch (1993) as likely to promote transfer: first, individuals should see how they can apply what is being learned in a variety of contexts, and, second, they should be required to find these applications themselves. Similar positions on the conditions that promote transfer have been taken by McDaniel and Schlager (1990), Robins and Mayer (1993), and others. In our research, subjects worked simultaneously on multiple problems that bore no relation with respect to surface content but were identical in structure and required the same strategies for successful solution. In addition, their activity within each problem domain was self-directed. A question that the present data do not resolve is whether simultaneous engagement with multiple problems is a necessary condition for transfer, as Sternberg and Frensch (1993) suggest it may be. Specifically, would our transfer results have been comparable had subjects worked on only a single problem at a time? Additional research is necessary to answer this question.

### *Variability, Generality, and Change*

Although the transfer findings establish generality of strategies, cross-domain variability, or specificity, was evident, some of it systematic. For example, performance was poorer in the social domain—a difference to which we return. This opposition between generality and specificity points to distinctions that sometimes fail to be made between generality in the *applicability* of strategies, generality in the *competence* to use them, and generality in their actual *application*. Each of these types of generality assumes the preceding one. The first, applicability, does not rest on empirical data. We chose to study strategies of broad applicability, whereas we might have chosen ones specific to particular content, for example, strategies for playing tic-tac-toe or chess. The second and third types of generality depend on answers to empirical questions. Does an individual who acquires competence to use a strategy in one domain also acquire competence to use it in another (the second type)? Does an individual having such competence apply the strategy consistently in all contexts in which it is applicable (the third type)? Our transfer results (as well as our data on initial emergence of strategies) indicate a positive answer to the first question, whereas our data showing multiple strategy usage indicate a negative answer to the second.

What are the implications of our findings of variability and generality with respect to the process of development? The generality findings confirm that it is something general that is developing—changing knowledge was confined to the particular domain in which it occurred, but the same was not true of strategies. Although their attention was focused on boats or TV programs, our subjects were developing much more broadly applicable kinds of competencies (even if they exhibited them only inconsistently).

The evidence of variability greatly complicates the picture of what it is that is changing. Rather than a simple unidimensional transition, the change process must be conceptualized in terms of multiple strategies each following separate (although not independent) paths of development—paths that may involve decline or stability as well as increase in frequency of usage. We return to the process of change later in this chapter, after our data on change have been summarized.

## MICROGENETIC ANALYSIS OF CHANGE

### *Microgenetic Change Compared across Age Groups*

Cross-sectional comparisons of performance across age groups can be misleading since they are susceptible to the limitations of single-session assessment that have already been discussed. Comparisons based on microgenetic assessment are potentially more informative since groups can be compared not just with respect to absolute level of initial performance but in terms of the form of change as well as the plasticity, or range of improvement, that they show. The child sample in the present study was the one in the normative age range for emergence of the kinds of strategies examined, yet the adult sample showed more progress, and hence plasticity, in response to identical forms and amounts of exercise. Overall, neither children's strategy development nor their final levels of attainment equaled that of adults. Nor did children gain as much knowledge as adults did within the individual content domains, thus supporting the connection between strategies and knowledge acquisition. Our data, then, provide no evidence of a "critical period" in childhood or adolescence following which the capacity for change is diminished. Variability may provide the raw material from which change arises (Siegler, 1994), as we discuss further later, but there is no evidence that such processes are confined to childhood.

Alongside the differences in performance of the two age groups are important commonalities. Strategy development appeared to follow the same general course in children and adults, as we review in more detail shortly. In addition to the common characteristic of intraindividual variability that has already been highlighted, another equally notable characteristic common to both groups is interindividual variability. One child showed overall performance superior to that of any of the adults, and by the end of the observation period several adults had reached no more advanced a level than many of the children. Consonant, then, with the absence of a critical period for change among individuals of preadolescent age and beyond, there appear to be no strong developmental constraints with respect to the time of emergence or consolidation of the skills examined in this *Monograph,* with some individuals clearly progressing sooner, faster, or further than others of a similar chronological age.

A possible criticism of our comparison of change across the two age groups is that it is compromised by a lack of initial equivalence of the two groups. Except for the one child with perfect validity of inference, subjects of both age groups showed a low initial level of valid inference. Still, even within the first session, the adults as a group were overall performing at a higher level than the children, raising the possibility that differences in achievement across the sessions should be attributed to preexisting differences between the two groups.

A methodology that we might have pursued would have been to attempt to match children and adults more precisely with respect to initial level. The pitfalls of this technique have been well characterized by Stigler and Miller (1993). "A good match is hard to find," they note, because, even if one can be found, in seeking out subjects identical on certain dimensions to those from an unselected older or younger age group the researcher is isolating individuals who are less and less representative of their own age group. As a result, the matched subjects are bound to differ from the unselected comparison age group on a host of other (unmatched) dimensions that the researcher can neither identify nor control for. All these uncontrolled dimensions stand to confound the interpretation of subsequent performance differences—exactly the outcome the researcher was seeking to avoid in employing the matching technique.

The approach that we have taken instead is to study younger and older subjects who come from the same broad demographic population and who as far as we can tell are representative of their respective age groups within this population. Earlier cross-sectional work (Kuhn et al., 1988) indicated that we could readily find preadolescents and adults who were similar, although not necessarily identical, in initial proficiency in the kinds of cognitive skills of concern to us, making it feasible to compare their respective courses of change. The results could have turned out the opposite, with children showing greater progress (an outcome having very different implications). Instead, the results that we did obtain show that the adults' zone of proximal development, to use Vygotsky's (1978) concept, was (on average) greater than the children's. Initial differences between the two groups, whatever their exact magnitude, were not striking—indeed they were substantially smaller than within-group differences—and by no means were they large enough to explain the sizable differences between the two groups by the time of the final session.

Although preexisting differences between groups in the skills that we assess cannot explain subsequent differences in their performance, the conclusion is nonetheless obviously correct that other differences between the groups existed—differences, moreover, that contributed to their respective performance. Adults and children looked roughly similar at the outset, yet there was obviously something—indeed, most likely a great many things—different about the adults that allowed them to profit to a greater extent (in terms of both knowledge and strategies) from the experience than did the children. This was, at least in part, what we undertook the study to find out.

Process analyses of representative samples from different points in the life cycle with respect to the same sequence of development offer the means to gain further insight into such differences in developmental potential. Schauble's research (Schauble, in press; Schauble & Glaser, 1990) warrants mention in this respect since she has undertaken comparisons of children and adults engaged in scientific investigation that are similar to the present one in a number of respects. Adults in her studies include both college students (Schauble & Glaser, 1990) and middle-aged adults employed in clerical and custodial positions (Schauble, in press). In both cases, the children are similar in age to those in the present work. The study that has a microgenetic component (Schauble, in press) was undertaken concurrently with the present work and involves problem content that is similar but confined to the physical science domain. Subjects in both age groups worked on two problems sequentially, rather than simultaneously as in the present work, in six sessions over a 2-week period. Although Schauble's focus in analyzing these data differs somewhat from ours and she does not address the issue of transfer, her data corroborate the major findings that we have reported. Both age groups showed variable strategy usage, both groups improved, but adults outperformed children overall.

### *Does Microgenetic Change Resemble Naturally Occurring Change?*

The question of comparability of change across the two age groups leads to another question. To what extent is change observed microgenetically comparable to naturally occurring change? The utility of the microgenetic method is dependent on the answer to this question. How can this comparability be evaluated? To the extent that microgenetic experience in applying strategies resembles naturally occurring experience (except for its density), we can have more confidence that processes of change in the two contexts have similar characteristics. Multivariable inductive inference is commonplace in everyday experience, as discussed in Chapter I, and we designed the microgenetically observed activity to resemble naturally occurring experience in other respects discussed earlier. True, our interviewers asked subjects numerous questions that subjects might not ask themselves ("What did you find out?" "How do you know?"), but the purpose was to get them to exercise inference strategies that otherwise would not get exercised, or at least not exercised as frequently. In other words, the purpose of these questions was to promote the use of strategies, not to influence their nature by means of feedback or instruction.

It can be claimed, then, that our intervention simply increased the density of naturally occurring experience. This is not the case, however, in all uses of the microgenetic method. Other investigators have experimented with more directive forms of a microgenetic method and obtained results similar to ours in certain key respects, such as the prevalence of mixed strategy usage. The microgenetic method thus appears robust across such variations, from our nondirective technique at one end of a continuum to more directive methods at the other. For example, a structured sequence of highly specific problems is presented (White, 1993), subjects are given feedback regarding the correctness of their strategies (Siegler, 1995), or new strategies are modeled that the subject is asked to evaluate (Siegler, 1995). The latter instances represent interventions intermediate between the microgenetic method as we define it here and a more traditional training study extended over time.

Although focused squarely on process (unlike early training studies), the latter uses of the microgenetic method raise the core training-study question of whether this is the way change *can* happen or the way it *does* happen in natural settings (Kuhn, 1974). Like results of earlier well-done training studies, Siegler's (1995) comparison of the effectiveness of different forms of intervention is informative in its own right and suggests the value of microgenetic analysis for this purpose. But the primary objective of this use of the microgenetic method is not to simulate a natural process of change.

In microgenetic studies in which this simulation is the primary goal, the broad criterion by which success in achieving this goal can be evaluated is the extent to which various features of the microgenetic change process resemble those of the natural change process. In the case of cognitive skills that are not normally the object of direct instruction, such as conservation in Siegler's (1995) case or the knowledge acquisition strategies examined in the present work, the role that the experimenter plays in interacting with the subject is a particularly important feature and one under the researcher's direct control. The most important feature not under the researcher's control is the extent to which the form and direction of change resemble those observed (in less detail) in cross-sectional studies. Comparison of the present findings with cross-sectional data (Kuhn et al., 1988) is positive in this respect. In addition, our findings with respect to generality indicate that the changes that the microgenetic method induces are at least as broadly based as changes that might be observed in natural settings. In sum, although we cannot be certain of total comparability, the indications are positive enough to make the microgenetic method a promising technique in studying processes of developmental change.

## THE MICROGENETIC STUDY OF PROCESSES OF KNOWLEDGE ACQUISITION

Until now we have discussed implications of our microgenetic research with respect to cognitive strategies and strategy change in general. In this section, we turn to the particular strategies that were the focus of the present work. Beginning with Kuhn and Phelps (1982), our microgenetic research has all been conducted within a paradigm in which subjects are asked to investigate a multivariable domain and make inductive inferences. The paradigm elicits cognitive strategies that are of broad application but not necessarily representative of all cognitive strategies, and replication of the findings reported here with other kinds of cognitive strategies would be desirable.

Yet our paradigm serves in many respects as a particularly fruitful one for microgenetic investigation. As discussed in Chapter II, it provides the subject a functional goal, particularly important in the case of repeated engagement with a task, and it offers the researcher the opportunity for the parallel observation of change on two planes—developing knowledge and the strategies by which this knowledge is acquired. A further advantage is that our problems are well suited to capture the dynamic of competition among strategies, a core aspect of what microgenetic analysis reveals. Largely because of the explanatory freedom that it allows, our problem format offers a rich opportunity to observe such competition. As we saw in Chapter VII, if an outcome appears to conflict with a subject's expectations with respect to one variable, these implications can be avoided simply by shifting to other variables to do the explanatory work, even though this freedom most often carries a cost in the quality of the inference strategies that are applied. More adequate strategies are thus in constant competition with less adequate ones.

What has this use of the microgenetic method told us about processes of knowledge acquisition? Perhaps the most essential thing that our results indicate is what people definitely do *not* do in acquiring new knowledge, and that is simply to access and gradually accumulate evidence until they feel that they have enough to draw a conclusion. Instead, theoretical beliefs shape the evidence that is examined, the way in which that evidence is interpreted, and the conclusions that are drawn. The subjects reported on in this *Monograph* drew conclusions virtually from the outset, on the basis of minimal or no data, and then changed their minds repeatedly, with even valid inclusions and exclusions by no means settling the question of the role that a particular feature plays. The challenge that the individual faces is one, then, not simply of correctly "reading" the data, but of coordinating theories and evidence. New knowledge does not simply add to or displace existing knowledge; new and old must be coordinated and reconciled. It is in this framework of theory-evidence coordination that the process of knowledge acquisition needs to be conceptualized and studied.

Knowledge acquisition strategies improve with practice, we have seen, in both groups studied. Shortly, we examine what insight our microgenetic data provide regarding this improvement. Yet the most puzzling question raised by our findings is perhaps not why (and how) strategies improve but rather why they don't improve more than they do. In Chapter I, we reviewed studies demonstrating early developments in skills that are clearly entailed in the problems that our subjects confronted—representation of belief states, distinguishing between determinate and indeterminate situations, distinguishing between a hypothesis and evidence bearing on it, inferring causality from covariation, and even control of variables. We can presume that the adults in our sample had been in possession of the early developing competencies reviewed in Chapter I for many years. How could it be, then, that, as they repeatedly examined a well-structured, determinate database of limited complexity, so many of them remained so oblivious to the implications of simple patterns of covariation and noncovariation evidence? It is this failure that is perhaps more remarkable than the evidence of early forms of competence reviewed in Chapter I.

The question does not have one simple answer. Compared to tasks involved in the studies of early competence reviewed in Chapter I, our tasks require more complex forms of strategic, metastrategic, and metacognitive competence, to which we turn in the next section. In addition, affective investment is a contributing factor. In the studies described in Chapter I, propositions were deliberately chosen as ones regarding which subjects would be unlikely to have any prior belief or preference (e.g., whether some dolls prefer red or green food). In our paradigm, in contrast, subjects are engaged in reasoning about the bearing of evidence on theories that are their own and to which they have in the immediate setting publicly committed themselves.

In our view, however, the explanation of poor performance lies not just in subject variables of cognitive skill or affective investment but also in the task variable of the freedom that the task allows. Subjects are free to choose how they wish to approach the tasks that we present them. They examine as much or as little of the database as they choose to, and only those data that are attended to need be explained. Subjects decide when they will make inferences and what inferences they will make; they are never required to draw determinate conclusions. Coupled with this freedom afforded by the task format is the freedom deriving from the fact that subjects have available multiple inference strategies that make it possible for them to justify just about any conclusion they wish. Much psychological research exists demonstrating the reasoning competencies that subjects display in highly structured tasks that require them to choose between two alternatives or make some similarly determinate form of response. In the present work, we see the different picture that emerges when subjects have the freedom to organize how they will approach and execute a task—an undertaking, moreover, that is extended over time, allowing even greater opportunity to choose how to allocate attention and effort.

It is exactly this freedom extended over time that is characteristic of inductive causal inference in natural settings. Our situation also resembles a real-world one in that new information bears on a diversity of theories to which one is committed and can therefore be drawn on in multiple ways. Most notable about our results, then, is the evidence of suboptimal application of strategies when individuals are in situations like these that allow them the freedom to structure their own cognitive activity. Despite displaying the strategic competence to reason more rigorously on occasion, subjects do not utilize this competence effectively in a way that would optimize their performance. In the next section, we examine the missing or insufficiently developed competencies that may have prevented subjects from making better use of the freedom that our task afforded.

## DEVELOPING COMPETENCIES

Despite the challenges that our problems posed to them, subjects used their less than perfect strategies to acquire knowledge, and over time these strategies improved. In this section, we examine the various kinds of competencies involved. We organize them under the three headings *strategic competence, metastrategic competence,* and *metacognitive competence* that were introduced in Chapter I.

### *Strategic Competence*

Strategic competence is competence to execute the investigative and inference strategies that yield valid conclusions. Among the adult sample, we saw that the basic strategies of valid intent, coordination of inference and intent, evidence-based inference, use of comparative (two-instance) evidence, controlled comparison, and valid inclusion and exclusion inference were largely in place in subjects' repertories, even if they were exercised only infrequently; the major change observed was in the ratio of usage of valid and invalid strategies. This was not always the case in the child sample, and we return to issues surrounding the emergence of these strategies when they are initially absent.

Among adults, more complex strategies (involving coordination of multiple factors) were not always within the subject's competence, as we saw in Chapters V and VII. Yet the more important finding is that, even when strategic competence is well in place, strategies are not consistently applied. This finding highlights the fact that more is involved in competent performance than ability to execute correct strategies.

### *Metastrategic Competence*

A second component of competence is metastrategic competence. It is highlighted in tasks like the one we have examined in which subjects must select the strategies they will apply. What makes metastrategic understanding critical is that it, and not strategic competence, dictates the strategies that are used. The distinction between strategic and metastrategic competence is that between knowing how to execute a strategy and understanding its significance (Kuhn, 1983; Moshman, 1990). Metastrategic competence includes understanding of both the value and the limitations of a strategy—in practical terms, of knowing how, when, and why the strategy should be used. In the case of the controlled comparison strategy central to the present work, metastrategic understanding includes a recognition of its necessity if the resulting inferences are to be valid, a recognition not implied by the mere use of the strategy. To the contrary, continued use of uncontrolled comparison and invalid inference in conjunction with valid strategies implies that this necessity is not recognized.

Metastrategic competence applies to invalid strategies as well as valid ones. It must be recognized why they don't work, or why they work inefficiently, if the ever-present temptation to succumb to them is to be resisted. The major change observed over time among our adult sample was inhibition of invalid false inclusion strategies, a factor clearly under the influence of metastrategic factors. The use of valid strategies thus implies neither an understanding of the need to use them nor an awareness of the pitfalls of resorting to less adequate strategies; metastrategic competence is implicated in both.

Yet a third aspect of metastrategic competence has to do with understanding the task. Strategies are applied in the service of the goals and purposes of particular tasks. Features of potential strategies must be coordinated with features of the task to yield skilled performance. We can think of a set of strategies appropriate to a task and another overlapping set of strategies within the repertory of a subject approaching the task. To perform successfully, the subject must coordinate the two sets and select an intersecting subset that will be applied—a requirement that entails the metastrategic understanding of both sets. Part of the task aspect of metastrategic understanding is a higher-order understanding of the overall task structure and goals—a framework within which task-relevant strategies are organized. If this understanding is weak or absent, performance is bound to suffer. In the case of our task, for example, we saw that most subjects lacked a sophisticated representation of the structure of the task as involving potentially additive and interactive effects of multiple variables; even more fundamentally, some subjects had difficulty maintaining a focus on the task goal of understanding the causal status of particular features (in contrast to producing desired outcomes).

### *Metacognitive Competence*

In contrast to metastrategic competence, which has to do with the form of one's knowledge, metacognitive competence involves reflection on its content. Everyone thinks with their theories, but they do not necessarily think about them. The task in which our subjects engaged requires strong metacognitive competencies since it focuses on justifying assertions by identifying and retaining knowledge of their sources (the bases for claiming them to be true)—an accomplishment involving differentiation of theory and evidence at a metacognitive level. In its absence, representations of theory and evidence may be merged into a single representation of "the way things are" since the sources of this knowledge are not distinguished.

Whether subjects regard the evidence that has been accessed as legitimate or consequential enough to warrant revision of their own theories is not the issue at stake. A metacognitively competent subject who is dismissive of the evidence, just like one who is more accepting of it, will be able to recognize its implications—what it implies with respect to a theory the subject holds (or does not hold). These implications will be recognized equally readily in the case in which the evidence is consonant with the theory and in the case in which it contradicts the theory. How the subject chooses to resolve the discrepancy in the latter case is not crucial. What is critical is that the implications of new evidence are processed and represented as an entity, independent of belief, which also must be represented as a distinct entity and compared to the representation of evidence.

Contrast this portrayal of competent metacognitive functioning with the examples that we presented of subjects such as Carmen and Maria, who appeared to have only the dimmest awareness of their theories as belief states subject to disconfirmation. When discrepant evidence accumulated, neither Carmen nor Maria acknowledged it as discrepant with her theory, as the more competent subject would have. Instead, both subjects marshaled fragments of this evidence (both single instances and comparisons) as *supporting* the theory rather than conflicting with it. Rather than compare evidence to theory, they used available evidence to *illustrate* what from their perspective they knew to be true.

As a consequence, the metacognitive distinction between theory- and evidence-based justification remained blurred, as it did for many subjects. When theory-based justifications are offered in response to questions about the implications of evidence, individuals are likely to have only limited awareness of the bases for the beliefs they hold. In the case of the humor feature, Maria's theory, we saw, evolved from causal to noncausal, yet she evidenced no awareness of any role played by the evidence that she had examined in effecting this shift. In Carmen's struggle with the humor feature, theory- and evidence-based justification merged in the service of a common end, leaving her certain of her causal belief but not metacognitively aware with regard to its source. We thus see in our adult subjects the critical significance that maintaining metacognitive awareness of the sources of one's beliefs—a skill examined in its most elementary forms in studies reviewed in Chapter I—comes to have.

It should be emphasized that the role of metacognitive competence is not limited to contexts in which personal beliefs are salient as a threat to "objective" processing. Metacognitive competencies figure to varying degrees in most forms of cognitive activity. Even in the case of psychological tasks deliberately constructed to be as "knowledge lean" as possible, the material on which the subject is asked to act (even if no more than so-called meaningless symbols), as well as the context in which it is presented, holds some meaning for the subject, and this meaning shapes subsequent processing.

Finally, metacognitive distancing from one's theories is not a routine achievement but an ideal that even professional scientists fall short of (Mahoney, 1976; Nissani & Hoefler-Nissani, 1992). Throughout their lives, even the most cognitively competent adults remain challenged to justify to themselves and others why they believe what they do and to be aware of the sources of their beliefs. They remain challenged to bring evidence to bear on their beliefs in a way that reflects clear differentiation between the implications of evidence and what they believe to be true. The inclination to draw on available evidence to illustrate what one believes to be true is always present.

## THE DEVELOPMENTAL COURSE OF KNOWLEDGE ACQUISITION AS THEORY-EVIDENCE COORDINATION

The children in our sample did not perform as well overall as did the adults, and their comparative deficiencies extended across strategic competencies (e.g., the use of multiple-instance evidence), metastrategic competencies (e.g., the inhibition of local interpretation and false inclusion), and metacognitive competencies (e.g., the conflation of evidence- and theory-based justification). Yet both groups showed progress along a similar course. Broadly, the case study and quantitative data taken together suggest a progression that begins with an awareness of the evidence being generated as relevant to the assertions being made, a prerequisite to the differentiation of theory- and evidence-based justification of these assertions. Once evidence begins to be referenced as justification, single instances are likely to be invoked to support a theoretical claim, with theory- and evidence-based justification sometimes merged. For example, the subject notices that, in the instance in front of him or her, music was indeed present and the show was popular, just as it should be according to the subject's belief in this feature's causal power.

Soon, a contrasting instance is likely to arise (perhaps constructed deliberately, perhaps not) in which the absence of music co-occurs with a poor outcome, and the subject realizes that this instance similarly can bolster the claim. Once this use of single-instance evidence becomes consolidated, the progression to linking these single instances into two-instance comparisons is not difficult, beginning most likely simply with the recollection of a previous instance. While interpreting a positive feature level and a positive outcome as supporting a causal theory, for example, the subject adds to the interpretation ". . . and before, when we didn't have it, it came out bad."

Once the utility of co-occurrence and covariation evidence in corroborating theoretical claims is recognized, the subject is likely to begin to attend to the evidence more consistently, with a corresponding decline in the frequency of theory-based justification. Because of their critical role in the development of valid inference, of particular significance is the emergence of multiple-instance evidence-based justifications. However, in the form described thus far, these multiple-instance inferences are limited to contexts in which theory and data are consonant, and they are focused on causal theories, with features believed noncausal more likely to be simply dismissed on theoretical grounds and not related to evidence. Evidence-based inclusion inferences may include generalized inferences over a larger number of instances, but only if the subject has the theoretical motivation to note these broader patterns. In short, these inferences remain theory motivated, uncontrolled, and as a consequence invalid. They function largely in the role of theory-protective devices and promote the fallacious use of data.

To progress beyond this point, competencies of all three kinds are necessary. Metastrategic competence is needed to inhibit the "local interpretation" of isolated instances and to lead the subject to look for patterns over larger segments of the database. Achieving this milestone requires strategic competence in data interpretation (particularly with respect to exclusion), but it also requires the metacognitive competence to reflect on and thereby achieve distance from one's own theories—to "bracket" them sufficiently that they are not allowed to dictate the ways in which evidence is processed.

A single instance, and even an uncontrolled pair of instances, as we have seen, can be used as evidence to justify just about any conclusion one wishes. Larger segments of the database are more difficult to misuse if they are represented accurately. Metacognitive awareness of one's theories is essential, as we have seen, if one is to distinguish and contemplate the bearing that evidence has on them.

A final strategic hurdle is controlled comparison, allowing both valid exclusion and valid inclusion. Valid inferences are at first infrequent and increase only gradually, with consistent application of valid strategies an achievement that few subjects attain. In addition to the metacognitive competence entailed in the bracketing of theories, what appears to be missing is the metastrategic competence that governs the relinquishing of invalid strategies and the recognition of the effectiveness of valid ones. We discuss the development of controlled comparison further in the next section.

In the absence of the development that we have sketched here, new evidence may lead to theory change, but the process is not one that the individual is aware of or exercises conscious control over. Our microgenetic (as well as earlier cross-sectional) evidence for the progression described here stands as counterevidence to claims (Brewer & Samarapungavan, 1991; Carey, 1985a) that there is no evidence of fundamentally different forms of processing by immature, intuitive scientists and professional scientists. We turn now to the question of how and why development from one form to the other occurs.

## UNDERSTANDING THE CHANGE PROCESS

How change occurs is in some sense the quintessential developmental question. In much developmental literature, however, it has largely been reduced to a question of where new strategies come from. The emergence of new strategies is a legitimate issue that developmentalists must address; yet it appears to be only one part of a larger picture. As we have already noted, intraindividual variability considerably complicates the developmental picture. In particular, it reveals as inadequate a traditional disequilibrium model of change, in which an individual is portrayed as functioning at particular stage levels for prolonged periods with briefer periods of disequilibrium and vacillation marking the transition from one stage to another. If, in contrast, an individual is chronically in a state of vacillation or variable strategy usage, this state cannot by itself explain change.

If an individual at any one time has available a multiplicity of strategies, as our own and others' microgenetic data indicate, and if these strategies have varying strengths associated with them (in the sense of probability of usage), then developmental change can be characterized as changes in the respective strengths of each of these strategies, with the emergence of a new strategy appearing as an increase from a strength of zero and the abandonment of an old one as a decline to a level of zero over some period. Capturing the complex interactive changes that are involved is likely to necessitate dynamic systems models of change (Van Geert, 1991; Van der Maas & Molenaar, 1992).

Our organization of developing competencies into strategic, metastrategic, and metacognitive categories raises a further set of process questions. What is the developmental course of the three kinds of competencies? For example, to what extent do metastrategic competencies precede instead of follow strategic ones? Some classic work in the moral development literature suggested a hierarchy of first appreciation, then comprehension, and only later production of more advanced forms of understanding (Rest, Turiel, & Kohlberg, 1969). According to this framework, individuals will comprehend and appreciate more advanced reasoning than they themselves use. More recent work, however, suggests that this generalization is not entirely correct. In one of two studies, Siegler and Crowley (1994) obtained results consonant with such a sequence—children rated a more efficient strategy that was modeled for them more highly than one they themselves used in a tic-tac-toe game. In a similar study of simple arithmetic strategies, however, children gave low ratings to an incorrect strategy but gave no higher rating to a more efficient strategy than they did to their own less efficient (but correct) strategy. In this case, then, metastrategic awareness does not appear to precede strategic capability.

In her most recent microgenetic research involving preschoolers' work with a balance scale, Metz (1993) contrasts problem representation (an aspect of metastrategic competence) and problem-solving strategies. She suggests that developments in these respective realms interact with one another, even though development in one may not be a sufficient cause for development in the other. In a similar vein, the tentative conceptualization of process that we propose is that metastrategic understanding may both guide (in implicit form) and follow (in more explicit form) strategy development.

To focus on an example central to the present work, does a subject understand the value of the controlled comparison strategy in initially undertaking to apply it? Or does this understanding develop only afterward and gradually, as the subject observes the consistency and clarity of the conclusions that the strategy allows? The gradual increase in frequency of usage suggests a gradually increasing awareness of the strategy's power. For this development to occur, however, the strategic achievement of at least some use of the strategy must occur, and the subject must also have metastrategic awareness of having used the strategy.

A further prerequisite is sufficient task-oriented metastrategic development to recognize the need to focus on the effect of a single feature at a time (a strategy that controlled comparison guarantees). This task-oriented metastrategic understanding may boost development of controlled comparison by reducing the subject's attention to other variables. In the traditional formal operations literature, failure to control other variables is attributed to inattention to them, with the result that they are allowed to vary randomly. An alternative explanation, one that becomes more likely when subjects' theoretical involvement is high, is overattention (rather than underattention) to these variables, as the subject seeks to demonstrate (in a single pair of instances) all the effects believed to be operating. With increasing metastrategic understanding of the task goal of assessing the effect of one specific feature, the subject may cease to vary these other variables across two-instance comparisons because of an increasing sense that they are not relevant to the comparison being made. Once they are left alone (and thereby "neutralized," in Inhelder and Piaget's, 1958, terminology), the way is prepared for increased usage and increasing metastrategic understanding of the power of controlled comparison.

The most challenging strategic developments may be the ones for which there are no metastrategic "advance organizers" to function as scaffolding for what is to come. Isolation of simple causal and noncausal effects by means of valid inclusion and exclusion, for example, yields a certain closure. Once it is demonstrated, the subject is not disposed to replicate an effect at different levels of other variables (and hence is not exposed to the discrepant evidence that could result), and nothing occurs to promote metastrategic awareness of the possibility of interaction effects.

In conclusion, we are left with a dual answer to the question of why microgenetic exercise of strategies leads to change. Exercise is critical in perfecting the use of strategies, but repeated application is also likely to foster greater metastrategic awareness of them (an awareness, as we noted, that guides, as well as follows, further strategic development). The two kinds of change—strategic and metastrategic—most likely work in complementary fashion and reinforce one another. It is an overly simple conceptualization, then, to see change as triggered by a single, critical instance of discrepant feedback or disequilibrium. Consonant with this claim, analysis of the children's data showed the first appearance of a valid inference strategy to be equally likely to follow theory-consonant and theory-discrepant outcomes. And discrepant feedback, it must be kept in mind, need not lead to change or even be processed as such. It may lead to strategic regression as the subject turns to other features to try to make sense of an outcome. Or it may simply be cast aside: "I haven't found out anything," our subjects sometimes claimed, "because it didn't come out like I predicted." Equally as important as the inconsistencies produced by incorrect strategies may be the sense of effectiveness produced by correct strategies (Karmiloff-Smith, 1992). It may be this sense that ultimately causes them to "win out" over less effective ones (more than dissatisfaction with the latter).

A final topic that warrants mention in the discussion of the change process is the role of social factors, which are likely to be powerful in promoting change. Broadly speaking, reasoning in dialogic forms may be a particularly rich source of development of these same forms in interiorized, individual form (Damon, 1990; Kuhn, 1991; Moshman, 1995; Pontecorvo, 1993). The form of problem studied here is a particularly rich one for examining collaborative learning since subjects working together are likely to differ in content knowledge (i.e., the theories that they hold) as well as strategic and metastrategic knowledge. Content disagreements, in fact, offer one explanation of a mechanism that enables social collaboration to lead to a new level of understanding initially absent in all participants (Boom, 1991; Miller, 1987). In current work, we are studying pairs of subjects working together on the kinds of problems employed in the present research (while the subjects work alone on a parallel task on separate occasions). Their content disagreements appear to be a potent force in stimulating attention to strategy.

## REASONING IN SOCIAL AND PHYSICAL DOMAINS

The mention of social factors brings us to a topic not yet addressed—subjects' inferior performance in the social domain compared to that in the physical domain. The differences observed varied to some extent across the two samples, the most striking difference being for adults less accurate final theories in the social domain and for children inferior prediction of outcomes and a higher frequency of theory-based reasoning. For both groups, percentage of valid inference was consistently lower in the social domain, for all segments of both phases. These differences are notable, even though we cannot be sure of the causes underlying them. The fact that we designed and presented two different problems in the social domain and two in the physical domain gives us more confidence in specifying the nature of the difference between the two kinds of problems than we would have if only one problem in each domain had been involved. Nevertheless, without examining a wider range of problems within each domain, we cannot identify with certainty the critical features that differentiate the two domains, beyond noting that one deals with the actions and reactions of humans and the other with inanimate objects.

Differences in ease of reasoning about the two kinds of phenomena can be interpreted in both cognitive and affective terms. Subjects are likely to have a rich and varied array of existing theories in the social domain, with numerous inconsistencies both within and between theories (Turiel, Hildebrandt, & Wainryb, 1991). They are also likely to have affective investment in these theories. Both factors make the process of coordinating theories and evidence more challenging. The combination of high affect and high information may translate into a phenomenological state of conviction about one's own thinking that is stronger in the case of social than nonsocial phenomena. Both children and adults are likely to feel a conviction that they know what makes TV shows enjoyable more than they do what makes a difference in the speed of boats or cars. Although our work is suggestive in pointing to the likelihood of a difference in processing new evidence in social and nonsocial domains, further research is needed to specify the differences more precisely and to identify how cognitive and affective factors operate and, most likely, interact.

A difference that bears a connection to the social-physical difference is that between frequency of causal and noncausal inference—a difference, recall, that was greater in the social domain and greater among children than adults. If a subject operated exclusively with valid strategies, this difference would not occur. The effects in each of our problems were roughly evenly divided between causal and noncausal effects (since interactive and curvilinear effects reflected a combination of the two). Ideally, the controlled comparisons that precede valid inference are undertaken precisely to determine whether the inference to be drawn is one of inclusion or exclusion; it is the outcome that should determine which inference is made.

Yet subjects overall made many more inferences of inclusion than exclusion. This difference must be attributed to faulty strategies. Recall from Chapter I that generalized inclusion inference is more feasible in the case of inclusion than exclusion; overall, however, generalized inferences did not make up a large enough portion of the inference base to account for the difference in frequency between inclusion and exclusion. A more powerful factor is the fact that uncontrolled comparisons are more likely to yield differences in outcome (leading to inclusion inference) than equivalent outcomes (Chap. I). Coupled with this greater availability of data to support causal inferences is the fact that, like theories in the social compared to the physical domain, causal theories are likely to have more affective and cognitive valence than noncausal theories, which may be scarcely represented at all. As a consequence, subjects have greater interest in investigating features that they believe to be causal, leading them to look for the readily available differences (across outcomes) to support causal theories rather than the equivalencies that would support noncausal inferences. Causal theories were thus easy to form when they were initially absent, promoted by the abundant opportunities to draw on fragments of the data for support, and, once formed, were hard to relinquish. We thus see the connection between the two differences—social/nonsocial and causal/noncausal—and can see why relinquishing causal theories in the social domain posed the most difficult and persistent challenge of all.

## SUMMARY AND PRACTICAL IMPLICATIONS

### *Building Bridges in the Study of Cognitive Development*

The work reported in this *Monograph* has been concerned with bridge building, at a number of levels. By focusing on the cognitive strategies involved in the process of theory revision, we hope to have paved the way for stronger connections between knowledge-based and strategy-based approaches to the study of cognitive development.

At another level, we hope to have contributed to the building of a stronger bridge between qualitative and quantitative methods of data analysis. Qualitative case study analysis deserves more respect and use than it receives from most developmental psychologists. Developmentalists share an interest in understanding individuals and how they develop over time; surely the study of individual cases has a place in meeting this objective. At the same time, use of such methods does not dictate that group analysis be abandoned. As we hope to have illustrated, qualitative and quantitative analysis can be used in complementary ways that enhance understanding beyond what would be achieved by either method alone. Very broadly speaking, one can tell us about the nature and frequency of a particular behavior within a group of individuals, isolated from the context of other behaviors. The other identifies the place of that behavior in a narrative account of an individual's meaning-making effort over time. Both kinds of information are essential to understanding the psychological significance of the behavior.

Still another bridge, and one of special interest to us, is that between research and application. We turn finally, then, to the educational implications of our work.

### *Linking Theory and Application*

The applied implications of our work are closely tied to its major theoretical implications, and this concluding section highlights both. The phenomena examined in this *Monograph* relate directly to how people reason informally about everyday issues (Kuhn, 1992b, 1993). They are also relevant to thinking and learning in more formal educational settings. Educators have paid considerable attention to the literature on conceptual change, exploring data on children's evolving conceptions within various domains and their implications for learning and teaching. The need to help students revise rather than simply replace existing theories has received particular attention. If this framework of evolving theories is to be taken seriously as a model for educators, it needs to include an understanding of the mechanisms whereby new evidence is encountered and coordinated with existing theories. It is toward this goal that the present work has been directed.

The most significant educational implication of the work presented in this *Monograph* derives from its most basic and possibly single most important result—that exercise of reasoning strategies can be a sufficient condition to effect their change. Sound thinking is a habit—a disposition (Perkins, Jay, & Tishman, 1993), not just a competence. Our results make clear that consistent application is at least as important as competence and that, if reasoning is practiced, consistency in application of sound strategies is likely to improve. This latter fact alone makes it important to engage in close study of the process by which this happens.

It does not follow that more directive interventions are inappropriate or ineffective. Two of us (Kuhn et al., 1992, study 2; Zohar, 1994) have in fact done work toward developing such techniques. The position we have taken is that a rich database on how the process of developmental change occurs naturally is a necessary foundation that should inform efforts to develop more directive techniques designed to promote change. The cognitive weaknesses observed in the present work underscore the educational importance of this effort.

Our other major findings similarly have applied as well as theoretical implications. The findings with respect to generality confirm that subjects were gaining proficiency in broadly applicable kinds of skills, at the same time as their attention was focused on particular information about cars, boats, school, or television. These skills are not manifested to an equal extent across age or population groups and are imperfectly developed in most people. They therefore warrant the attention of educators, especially given the evidence of their modifiability.

The striking intraindividual variability that we observed highlights the message to educators that a single initial performance may provide little indication of an individual's full repertory or potential. Interindividual variability indicates that neither is chronological age a reliable indicator of performance or potential. The variability that we observed implies that cognitive change entails more than a simple transition from state *a* to *b*—whether it occurs naturally or under an educator's guidance. Multiple strategies and multiple forms of competence, including the metastrategic and the metacognitive, undergo simultaneous and interconnected development.

Particularly important for educators is the recognition of the role of metastrategic and metacognitive aspects of cognition in shaping performance, especially in situations like ours in which individuals have considerable freedom in structuring their own cognitive activity. Two practical implications stand out. One is the limited value of instruction aimed at teaching strategies if it does not include equal attention to the metastrategic understanding that determines if and where these strategies will be applied. The other is the need to develop means of teaching metastrategic and metacognitive awareness from an early age (Olson & Astington, 1993). Classroom discussions, for example, might be focused on possible bases for making a claim or on the relative merits of different strategies for solving a problem.

Finally, the differences that we observed between cognition in physical and social domains highlight the challenge that teachers face in simultaneously trying to engage their students and to promote their best thinking. Once they move beyond the "natural" curiosity of early childhood (Kuhn, 1992a), students often lose confidence in their capacity to understand the physical world. Topics in the social realm, in contrast, are attractive because they are easy to think about, as the result of much personal experience and accrued knowledge as well as affective investment and a metacognitive sense of knowledgeability—all of which work against the metacognitive distancing necessary for sound thinking. In short, topics in the social sphere both engage people and challenge them. They are easy to think about but hard to think well about. It is exactly this combination that warrants greater attention to them as vehicles for both studying and improving thinking.

# REFERENCES


Acredolo, C., & O'Connor, J. (1991). On the difficulty of detecting cognitive uncertainty. *Human Development,* **34,** 204–223.

Alloy, L., & Tabachnik, N. (1984). Assessment of covariation by humans and animals: The joint influence of prior expectations and current situational information. *Psychological Review,* **91,** 112–149.

Baltes, P. (1987). Theoretical propositions of life-span developmental psychology: On the dynamics between growth and decline. *Developmental Psychology,* **23,** 611–626.

Barrett, S., Abdi, H., Murphy, G., & Gallagher, J. (1993). Theory-based correlations and their role in children's concepts. *Child Development,* **64,** 1595–1616.

Bidell, T., & Fischer, K. (1994). Developmental transitions in children's early on-line planning. In M. Haith, J. Benson, & B. Pennington (Eds.), *The development of future-oriented processes.* Chicago: University of Chicago Press.

Bijou, S., & Baer, D. (1961). *Child development: A systematic and empirical theory.* New York: Appleton-Century-Crofts.

Boom, J. (1991). Collective development and the learning paradox. *Human Development,* **34,** 273–287.

Brewer, W., & Samarapungavan, A. (1991). Children's theories vs. scientific theories: Differences in reasoning or differences in knowledge? In R. Hoffman & D. Palermo (Eds.), *Cognition and the symbolic processes.* Hillsdale, NJ: Erlbaum.

Briggs, L. (1991). *Causal analysis and the induction of unobserved states and processes.* Unpublished doctoral dissertation, Columbia University. (Microfilm No. 9209789)

Brown, A. (1989). Analogical transfer: What develops? In S. Vosniadou & A. Ortony (Eds.), *Similarity and analogical reasoning.* New York: Cambridge University Press.

Brown, A. (1990). Domain-specific principles affect learning and transfer in children. *Cognitive Science,* **14,** 107–133.

Brown, A., & Kane, M. (1988). Preschool children can learn to transfer: Learning to learn and learning from examples. *Cognitive Psychology,* **20,** 493–523.

Bullock, M. (1985). Causal reasoning and developmental change over the preschool years. *Human Development,* **28,** 169–191.

Bullock, M., Gelman, R., & Baillargeon, R. (1982). The development of causal reasoning. In W. Friedman (Ed.), *The developmental psychology of time.* New York: Academic.

Byrnes, J., & Beilin, H. (1991). The cognitive basis of uncertainty. *Human Development,* **34,** 189–203.

Carey, S. (1985a). Are children fundamentally different kinds of thinkers and learners than adults? In S. Chipman, J. Segal, & R. Glaser (Eds.), *Thinking and learning skills* (Vol. **2**). Hillsdale, NJ: Erlbaum.

Carey, S. (1985b). *Conceptual change in childhood.* Cambridge, MA: MIT Press.

Carey, S. (1986). Cognitive science and science education. *American Psychologist,* **41,** 1123–1130.

Carey, S. (1990). Cognitive development. In D. Osherson & E. Smith (Eds.), *Thinking: An invitation to cognitive science.* Cambridge, MA: MIT Press.

Case, R. (1974). Structures and strictures: Some functional limitations on the course of cognitive growth. *Cognitive Psychology,* **6,** 544–573.

Cheng, P., & Nisbett, R. (1993). Pragmatic constraints on causal deduction. In R. Nisbett (Ed.), *Rules for reasoning.* Hillsdale, NJ: Erlbaum.

Cheng, P., & Novick, L. (1990). A probabilistic contrast model of causal induction. *Journal of Personality and Social Psychology,* **58,** 545–567.

Cheng, P., & Novick, L. (1991). Causes versus enabling conditions. *Cognition,* **40,** 83–120.

Cheng, P., & Novick, L. (1992). Covariation in natural causal induction. *Psychological Review,* **99**(2), 365–382.

Chi, M. (1992). Conceptual change within and across ontological categories: Examples from learning and discovery in science. In R. Giere (Ed.), *Cognitive models of science.* Minneapolis: University of Minnesota Press.

Damon, W. (1990). Social relations and children's thinking skills. In D. Kuhn (Ed.), *Developmental perspectives on teaching and learning thinking skills* (Contributions to Human Development, Vol. **21**). Basel: Karger.

Detterman, D. (1993). The case for the prosecution: Transfer as an epiphenomenon. In D. Detterman & R. Sternberg (Eds.), *Transfer on trial: Intelligence, cognition, and instruction.* Norwood, NJ: Ablex.

Detterman, D., & Sternberg, R. (Eds.). (1993). *Transfer on trial: Intelligence, cognition, and instruction.* Norwood, NJ: Ablex.

Downing, C., Sternberg, R., & Ross, B. (1985). Multicausal inference: Evaluation of evidence in causally complex situations. *Journal of Experimental Psychology: General,* **114,** 239–263.

Dunbar, K., & Klahr, D. (1989). Developmental differences in scientific discovery strategies. In D. Klahr & K. Kotovsky (Eds.), *Complex information processing: The impact of Herbert A. Simon* (Proceedings of the 21st Carnegie-Mellon Symposium on Cognition). Hillsdale, NJ: Erlbaum.

Einhorn, J., & Hogarth, R. (1986). Judging probable cause. *Psychological Bulletin,* **99,** 3–19.

Feldman, C. (1992). The new theory of theory of mind. *Human Development,* **35,** 109–114.

Flavell, J. (1979). Metacognition and cognitive monitoring: A new area of cognitive-developmental inquiry. *American Psychologist,* **34,** 906–911.

Flavell, J. (1993). Young children's understanding of thinking and consciousness. *Current Directions in Psychological Science,* **2,** 40–43.

Flavell, J. H., Green, F. L., & Flavell, E. R. (1995). Young children's knowledge about thinking. *Monographs of the Society for Research in Child Development,* **60**(1, Serial No. 243).

Flavell, J., & Wellman, H. (1977). Metamemory. In R. Kail & J. Hagen (Eds.), *Perspectives on the development of memory and cognition.* Hillsdale, NJ: Erlbaum.

Forrest-Pressley, D., MacKinnon, G., & Waller, T. G. (Eds.). (1985). *Metacognition, cognition, and human performance* (Vols. **1, 2**). Orlando, FL: Academic.

Gelman, S., & Wellman, H. (in press). The acquisition of knowledge. In W. Damon (Series Ed.), D. Kuhn & R. Siegler (Vol. Eds.), *Handbook of child psychology: Vol.* **2.** *Cognitive, language, and perceptual development* (5th ed.). New York: Wiley.

Gentner, D. (1983). Structure-mapping: A theoretical framework for analogy. *Cognitive Science,* **7,** 155–170.

Gentner, D. (1989). The mechanisms of analogical learning. In S. Vosniadou & A. Ortony (Eds.), *Similarity, analogy, and thought.* Cambridge: Cambridge University Press.

Gopnik, A., & Astington, J. (1988). Children's understanding of representational change and its relation to the understanding of false belief and the appearance-reality distinction. *Child Development,* **59,** 26–37.

Gopnik, A., & Graf, P. (1988). Knowing how you know: Young children's ability to identify and remember the sources of their beliefs. *Child Development,* **59,** 1366–1371.

Gopnik, A., & Slaughter, V. (1991). Young children's understanding of changes in their mental states. *Child Development,* **62,** 98–110.

Granott, N. (1993). Patterns of interaction in the co-construction of knowledge: Separate minds, joint effort, and weird creatures. In R. Wozniak & K. Fischer (Eds.), *Development in context: Acting and thinking in specific environments.* Hillsdale, NJ: Erlbaum.

Greeno, J., Smith, D., & Moore, J. (1993). Transfer of situated learning. In D. Detterman & R. Sternberg (Eds.), *Transfer on trial: Intelligence, cognition, and instruction.* Norwood, NJ: Ablex.

Hatano, G. (1994). Special-topic section: Japanese perspectives on conceptual change: Introduction. *Human Development,* **37**(4), 189–197.

Hilton, D., & Slugoski, B. (1986). Knowledge-based causal attribution: The abnormal conditions focus model. *Psychological Review,* **93,** 75–88.

Holland, J., Holyoak, K., Nisbett, R., & Thagard, P. (1986). *Induction: Processes of inference, learning, and discovery.* Cambridge, MA: MIT Press.

Holyoak, K. (1984). Analogical thinking and human intelligence. In R. Sternberg (Ed.), *Advances in the psychology of human intelligence* (Vol. **2**). Hillsdale, NJ: Erlbaum.

Holyoak, K., Koh, K., & Nisbett, R. (1989). A theory of conditioning: Inductive learning within rule-based default hierarchies. *Psychological Review,* **96**(2), 315–340.

Inhelder, B., & Piaget, J. (1958). *The growth of logical thinking from childhood to adolescence.* New York: Basic. (Original work published 1955)

Inhelder, B., & Piaget, J. (1969). *The early growth of logic in the child.* New York: Norton. (Original work published 1959)

Karmiloff-Smith, A. (1984). Children's problem solving. In M. Lamb, A. Brown, & B. Rogoff (Eds.), *Advances in developmental psychology* (Vol. **3**). Hillsdale, NJ: Erlbaum.

Karmiloff-Smith, A. (1992). *Beyond modularity: A developmental perspective on cognitive science.* Cambridge, MA: MIT Press.

Karmiloff-Smith, A. (1994). Precis of *Beyond modularity:* A developmental perspective on cognitive science (with multiple commentaries). *Behavioral and Brain Sciences,* **17**(4), 693–745.

Karmiloff-Smith, A., & Inhelder, B. (1974). If you want to get ahead, get a theory. *Cognition,* **3,** 195–212.

Keating, D. (1980). Thinking processes in adolescence. In J. Adelson (Ed.), *Handbook of adolescent psychology.* New York: Wiley.

Keil, F. (1988). Commentary. *Human Development,* **31,** 35–43.

Keil, F. (1989). *Concepts, kinds, and cognitive development.* Cambridge, MA: Bradford.

Keil, F. (1991). The emergence of theoretical beliefs as constraints on concepts. In S. Carey & R. Gelman (Eds.), *The epigenesis of mind: Essays on biology and cognition.* Hillsdale, NJ: Erlbaum.

Kelley, H. (1967). Attribution theory in social psychology. In D. Levine (Ed.), *Nebraska Symposium on Motivation* (Vol. **15**). Lincoln: University of Nebraska Press.

Kendler, H., & Kendler, T. (1975). From discrimination learning to cognitive development: A neobehavioristic odyssey. In W. K. Estes (Ed.), *Handbook of learning and cognitive processes* (Vol. **1**). Hillsdale, NJ: Erlbaum.

Klahr, D., Fay, A., & Dunbar, K. (1993). Heuristics for scientific experimentation: A developmental study. *Cognitive Psychology,* **25,** 111–146.

Kuhn, D. (1974). Inducing development experimentally: Comments on a research paradigm. *Developmental Psychology,* **10,** 590–600.

Kuhn, D. (1983). On the dual executive and its significance in the development of developmental psychology. In D. Kuhn & J. Meacham (Eds.), *On the development of developmental psychology* (Contributions to Human Development, Vol. **8**). Basel: Karger.

Kuhn, D. (1989). Children and adults as intuitive scientists. *Psychological Review,* **96,** 674–689.

Kuhn, D. (1991). *The skills of argument.* New York: Cambridge University Press.

Kuhn, D. (1992a). Piaget's child as scientist. In H. Beilin & P. Pufall (Eds.), *Piaget: Prospects and possibilities.* Hillsdale, NJ: Erlbaum.

Kuhn, D. (1992b). Thinking as argument. *Harvard Educational Review,* **62,** 155–178.

Kuhn, D. (1993). Connecting scientific and informal reasoning. *Merrill-Palmer Quarterly,* **39**(1), 74–103.

Kuhn, D., Amsel, E., & O'Loughlin, M. (1988). *The development of scientific thinking skills.* San Diego: Academic.

Kuhn, D., & Brannock, J. (1977). Development of the isolation of variables scheme in experimental and "natural experiment" contexts. *Developmental Psychology,* **13,** 9–14.

Kuhn, D., & Ho, V. (1980). Self-directed activity and cognitive development. *Journal of Applied Developmental Psychology,* **1,** 119–133.

Kuhn, D., & Phelps, E. (1982). The development of problem-solving strategies. In H. Reese (Ed.), *Advances in child development and behavior* (Vol. **17**). New York: Academic.

Kuhn, D., Schauble, L., & Garcia-Mila, M. (1992). Cross-domain development of scientific reasoning. *Cognition and Instruction,* **9**(4), 285–327.

Kunda, Z. (1990). The case for motivated reasoning. *Psychological Bulletin,* **108,** 480–498.

Lawler, R. (1985). *Computer experience and cognitive development: A child's learning in a computer culture.* New York: Wiley.

Mackie, J. (1974). *The cement of the universe: A study of causation.* Oxford: Clarendon.

Mahoney, M. (Ed.). (1976). *Scientist as subject: The psychological imperative.* Cambridge, MA: Ballinger.

McDaniel, M., & Schlager, M. (1990). Discovery learning and transfer of problem-solving skills. *Cognition and Instruction,* **7**(2), 129–159.

Medin, D. (1989). Concepts and conceptual structure. *American Psychologist,* **44,** 1469–1481.

Mendelson, R., & Shultz, T. (1976). Covariation and temporal contiguity as principles of causal inference in young children. *Journal of Experimental Psychology,* **22,** 408–412.

Metcalfe, J., & Shimamura, A. (1994). *Metacognition: Knowing about knowing.* Cambridge, MA: MIT Press.

Metz, K. (1985). The development of children's problem solving in a gears task: A problem space perspective. *Cognitive Science,* **9,** 431–471.

Metz, K. (1993). Preschoolers' developing knowledge of the pan balance: From new representation to transformed problem solving. *Cognition and Instruction,* **11**(1), 31–93.

Mill, J. S. (1973). System of logic. In J. M. Robson (Ed.), *Collected works of John Stuart Mill* (Vols. **7–8**). Toronto: University of Toronto Press. (Original work published 1843)

Miller, M. (1987). Argumentation and cognition. In M. Hickmann (Ed.), *Social and functional approaches to language and thought.* New York: Academic.

Moshman, D. (1979). To really get ahead, get a metatheory. In D. Kuhn (Ed.), *Intellectual development beyond childhood* (New Directions for Child Development, No. 5). San Francisco: Jossey-Bass.

Moshman, D. (1990). The development of metalogical understanding. In W. Overton (Ed.), *Reasoning, necessity, and logic: Developmental perspectives.* Hillsdale, NJ: Erlbaum.

Moshman, D. (1995). Reasoning as self-constrained thinking. *Human Development,* **38**(1), 53–64.

Moshman, D. (in press). Cognitive development beyond childhood. In W. Damon (Series Ed.), D. Kuhn & R. Siegler (Vol. Eds.), *Handbook of child psychology: Vol.* **2.** *Cognitive, language, and perceptual development* (5th ed.). New York: Wiley.

Nissani, M., & Hoefler-Nissani, D. (1992). Experimental studies of belief dependence of observations and of resistance to conceptual change. *Cognition and Instruction,* **9**(2), 97–111.

Olson, D., & Astington, J. (1993). Thinking about thinking: Learning how to take statements and hold beliefs. *Educational Psychologist,* **28**(1), 7–23.

Perkins, D., Jay, E., & Tishman, S. (1993). Beyond abilities: A dispositional theory of thinking. *Merrill-Palmer Quarterly,* **39**(1), 1–21.

Perner, J. (1991). *Understanding the representational mind.* Cambridge, MA: MIT Press.

Piaget, J. (1950). *The psychology of intelligence.* London: Routledge & Kegan Paul.

Piaget, J. (1952). *The origins of intelligence.* New York: International Universities Press.

Piaget, J., & Garcia, R. (1991). *Toward a logic of meanings.* Hillsdale, NJ: Erlbaum. (Original work published 1987)

Pieraut–Le Bonniec, G. (1980). *The development of modal reasoning.* New York: Academic.

Pontecorvo, C. (1993). Forms of discourse and shared thinking. *Cognition and Instruction,* **11**(3–4), 189–196.

Rest, J., Turiel, E., & Kohlberg, L. (1969). Level of moral development as a determinant of preference and comprehension of moral judgments made by others. *Journal of Personality,* **69**(7), 225–252.

Richardson, K. (1992). Covariation analysis of knowledge representation: Some developmental studies. *Journal of Experimental Child Psychology,* **53,** 129–150.

Robins, S., & Mayer, R. (1993). Schema training in analogical reasoning. *Journal of Educational Psychology,* **85**(3), 529–538.

Ruffman, T., Perner, J., Olson, D., & Doherty, M. (1993). Reflecting on scientific thinking: Children's understanding of the hypothesis-evidence relation. *Child Development,* **64,** 1617–1636.

Schauble, L. (1990). Belief revision in children: The role of prior knowledge and strategies for generating evidence. *Journal of Experimental Child Psychology,* **49,** 31–57.

Schauble, L. (in press). The development of scientific reasoning in knowledge-rich contexts. *Developmental Psychology.*

Schauble, L., & Glaser, R. (1990). Scientific thinking in children and adults. In D. Kuhn (Ed.), *Developmental perspectives on teaching and learning thinking skills* (Contributions to Human Development, Vol. **21**). Basel: Karger.

Schauble, L., Klopfer, L., & Raghavan, K. (1991). Students' transition from an engineering model to a science model of experimentation. *Journal of Research in Science Teaching,* **28**(9), 859–882.

Schneider, W. (1985). Developmental trends in the metamemory-memory behavior relationship: An integrative review. In D. Forrest-Pressley, G. MacKinnon, & T. Waller (Eds.), *Metacognition, cognition, and human performance.* Orlando, FL: Academic.

Schustack, M. (1988). Thinking about causality. In R. Sternberg & E. Smith (Eds.), *The psychology of human thought.* Cambridge: Cambridge University Press.

Schustack, M., & Sternberg, R. (1981). Evaluation of evidence in causal inference. *Journal of Experimental Psychology: General,* **110,** 101–120.

Sedlak, A., & Kurtz, S. (1981). A review of children's use of causal inference principles. *Child Development,* **52,** 759–784.

Shultz, T. (1982). Rules of causal attribution. *Monographs of the Society for Research in Child Development,* **47**(1, Serial No. 194).

Shultz, T., & Mendelson, R. (1975). The use of covariation as a principle of causal analysis. *Child Development,* **46,** 394–399.

Siegler, R. (1994). Cognitive variability: A key to understanding cognitive development. *Current Directions in Psychological Science,* **3**(1), 1–4.

Siegler, R. (1995). How does change occur: A microgenetic study of number conservation. *Cognitive Psychology,* **28**(3), 225–273.

Siegler, R., & Crowley, K. (1991). The microgenetic method: A direct means for studying cognitive development. *American Psychologist,* **46**(6), 606–620.

Siegler, R., & Crowley, K. (1994). Constraints on learning in non-privileged domains. *Cognitive Psychology,* **27**(2), 194–226.

Siegler, R., & Jenkins, E. (1989). *How children discover new strategies.* Hillsdale, NJ: Erlbaum.

Sigel, I. (1993). The centrality of a distancing model for the development of representational competence. In R. Cocking & K. A. Renninger (Eds.), *The development and meaning of psychological distance.* Hillsdale, NJ: Erlbaum.

Singley, M., & Anderson, J. (1989). *The transfer of cognitive skill.* Cambridge, MA: Harvard University Press.

Sodian, B., Zaitchik, D., & Carey, S. (1991). Young children's differentiation of hypothetical beliefs from evidence. *Child Development,* **62,** 753–766.

Sternberg, R. (Ed.). (1984). *Mechanisms of cognitive development.* New York: Freeman.

Sternberg, R. (1985). *Beyond IQ: A triarchic theory of human intelligence.* Cambridge: Cambridge University Press.

Sternberg, R., & Frensch, P. (1993). Mechanisms of transfer. In D. Detterman & R. Sternberg (Eds.), *Transfer on trial: Intelligence, cognition, and instruction.* Norwood, NJ: Ablex.

Stigler, J., & Miller, K. (1993). A good match is hard to find: Comment on Mayer, Tajika, and Stanley. *Journal of Educational Psychology,* **85**(3), 554–559.

Taylor, M., Esbensen, B., & Bennett, R. (1994). Children's understanding of knowledge acquisition: The tendency for children to report they have always known what they have just learned. *Child Development,* **65**(6), 1581–1604.

Turiel, E., Hildebrandt, C., & Wainryb, C. (1991). Judging social issues: Difficulties, inconsistencies, and consistencies. *Monographs of the Society for Research in Child Development,* **56**(2, Serial No. 224).

Van der Maas, H., & Molenaar, P. (1992). A catastrophe-theoretic approach to cognitive development. *Psychological Review,* **99,** 395–417.

Van Geert, P. (1991). A dynamic systems model of cognitive and language growth. *Psychological Review,* **98,** 3–53.

Vosniadou, S., & Brewer, W. (1987). Theories of knowledge restructuring in development. *Review of Educational Research,* **57,** 51–67.

Vosniadou, S., & Brewer, W. (1992). Mental models of the earth: A study of conceptual change in childhood. *Cognitive Psychology,* **24**(4), 535–585.

Vygotsky, L. S. (1978). *Mind in society: The development of higher psychological processes.* Cambridge, MA: Harvard University Press.

Wellman, H. (1990). *The child's theory of mind.* Cambridge, MA: MIT Press.

Wellman, H., & Gelman, S. (1992). Cognitive development: Foundational theories of core domains. *Annual Review of Psychology,* **43,** 337–375.

Werner, H. (1948). *Comparative psychology of mental development.* New York: International Universities Press.

White, B. (1993). Thinker tools: Causal models, conceptual change, and science education. *Cognition and Instruction,* **10**(1), 1–100.

White, S. (1994a). Commentary. *Human Development,* **37**(1), 36–41.

White, S. (1994b). Commentary. *Human Development,* **37**(2), 109–114.

Wisniewski, E., & Medin, D. (1994). On the interaction of theory and data in concept learning. *Cognitive Science,* **18,** 221–281.

Wohlwill, J. (1973). *The study of behavioral development.* New York: Academic.

Zohar, A. (1994). Teaching a thinking strategy: Transfer across domains and self-learning vs. classroom setting. *Applied Cognitive Psychology,* **8**(6), 549–564.

## ACKNOWLEDGMENTS

Parts of this work were supported by a grant to Deanna Kuhn from the National Science Foundation. Merce Garcia-Mila was supported by a Fullbright–La Caixa fellowship and a fellowship from CIRIT–Generelitat de Catalunya, Spain. Parts of the adult data were presented by Garcia-Mila in a dissertation submitted in fulfillment of requirements for the Ph.D. degree. Anat Zohar was supported by a Lady Davis fellowship and by a postdoctoral fellowship from the McDonnell Foundation. Christopher Andersen received predoctoral support from the National Science Foundation.

# COMMENTARY

## TOWARD AN EVOLUTIONARY EPISTEMOLOGY OF SCIENTIFIC REASONING

*Sheldon H. White*

Scientific reasoning has been the traditional high point or end point of children's cognitive development for many theorists. However, such reasoning has not been closely examined until recently, nor has it been shown to be unique among forms of human reasoning. Scientists reason carefully and precisely—sometimes, at least. Is the careful and precise reasoning of scientists different from careful and precise reasoning in business, law, administration, etc.? We do not know. Traditions have held scientific reasoning high as a sort of ideal for a long time. In the early 1800s, Auguste Comte argued that human sciences and societies pass through three historical stages: the theological, the metaphysical, and the positive (the scientific). Comte's three-stage conception of progress, by no means new with him, appealed to many educated people, and something like it was reexpressed in a subsequent stream of progressivist, evolutionist, and "social Darwinist" writings. Eventually, the conception of scientific thinking as an ideal found its way into theories saying that evolutionary progress is the fundamental movement in children's development—theories of cognitive development such as those by Romanes, Sechenov, Baldwin, Hall, and Piaget.

One meaningful activity of twentieth-century research in developmental psychology has been the periodic reconsideration of the psychologies of the past—the psychologies and ideologies in earlier philosophical writings, and the implicit psychologies sitting silently within the concepts, belief systems, and design institutions of modern society. This *Monograph* is addressed to a central, one might say a defining, phenomenon for traditional interpreters of children's cognitive development, the movement of the developing child toward the capacity for precise and careful scientific inference. Looking through the theoretical lenses of Jean Piaget, this phenomenon is seen as "the appearance of formal operations at adolescence, when second-order relations between categories begin to be examined—the skill on which the present *Monograph* focuses" (p. 11). As Piaget sees it, preadolescents become capable of formal operations when they engage in second-order operations, operations on operations, acquiring the metacognitive ability to take their own thought processes as objects of cognition.

Deanna Kuhn and her associates have mounted an active and powerful research program on scientific reasoning in adolescence. They have looked at how children come to make orderly, evidence-based inferences about what causes physical events (Kuhn, 1989a; Kuhn, Amsel, & O'Loughlin, 1988). They have asked how scientific and everyday reasoning differ (Kuhn, 1993a), how scientific reasoning and higher-order thinking skills can be taught (Kuhn, 1986, 1989b, 1990a, 1990b), and how reasoning about human activities compares with reasoning about physical events (Kuhn, Weinstock, & Flaton, 1994a, 1994b). Since scientific reasoning involves arguing, they have studied the organization of argument as an instrument of reason (Kuhn, 1992, 1993b; Kuhn et al., 1994a).

Research such as this has begun to show how adolescents perfect their scientific reasoning, while, curiously, other research has at the same time begun to show that elements of scientific reasoning are clearly there in childhood well before adolescence. The authors review the evidence for this in some detail. Very young children can entertain alternative possibilities, detect and interpret covariations, and isolate and control variables when they try to solve questions of causation. But these are partial capacities. Kuhn and her associates hold that the development of metacognitive competence takes place very gradually over many years and that this growth is accompanied by a steady increase in what Karmiloff-Smith calls "explication." As children grow older, they acquire more and more knowledges and procedures. They understand the capabilities and limits of their own thought processes more exactly. They acquire heuristics, tactics for problem solving. *Metacognitive* and *metastrategic* knowledges emerge. Metacognitive knowledge "involves awareness of and reflection on the content of one's thought, ranging from simple awareness of the content of one's present or immediately prior thought . . . to reflection on a set of propositions that one believes to be true or chooses to take under consideration." Metastrategic knowledge "involves awareness and management of the strategies that are applied in the course of thinking and problem solving" (p. 12).

Sophisticated scientific reasoning depends on the ability to differentiate theory from evidence very exactly and precisely, and this ability, in turn, depends on the availability and conscious control of both knowledges:

> If knowledge acquisition is a process of theory revision, as we have claimed, to accomplish the process in a skilled way the individual needs

> to be aware of and reflect on a theory (metacognitive competence), coordinating it with new evidence by means of strategies that are inferentially sound and applied in a consistent manner (metastrategic competence). In the total absence of such competence, evidence and theory are not represented as distinct entities. In this case, new evidence may lead to modification of a theory (as it does even among very young children), but the process takes place outside the individual's conscious control. (p. 12)

The fundamental problem for the research literature, the authors feel, is not the question of whether scientific reasoning is all there in the capacities children have in the early years but rather the question of why children, adolescents, and adults do not do better at scientific reasoning tasks: "A perplexing problem is to explain the persistent poor performance of children, adolescents, and many adults in full-fledged scientific reasoning tasks, that is, ones in which they are asked to examine a database and draw conclusions. . . . Addressing this critical question is an important objective of the present *Monograph*" (p. 16).

The study reported in this *Monograph* is a careful and extended microgenetic study of people arriving at causal inferences. The authors saw each of their subjects—fourth graders aged 8–10 and community college students aged 22–47—twice a week for 10 weeks. Each subject worked on one physical and one social problem for the first 5 weeks; then he or she switched to an alternative physical and social problem for the remaining 5 weeks. All problems were multivariable problems in which subjects had to estimate what kind of influence, if any, each of the five variables exerted on a class of phenomena. They watched a model boat sail along a tank repeatedly, estimating whether water depth, boat size, boat weight, sail color, and sail size were influencing the boat's speed. Looking at events presented to them in a computer microworld, they tried to estimate whether each of five factors was influencing the speed of a racing car. Pulling student records one by one out of a filing cabinet, they tried to estimate whether class size, classroom noisiness, sex of teacher, presence or absence of a teaching assistant, or teacher's availability during recess was influencing students' school performance. Pulling records of television programs one by one out of a filing cabinet, they tried to estimate whether program length, day of the week, presence or absence of humor, the use of music, or the presence of commercials was influencing the programs' ratings.

The specific problems used in the study are worth thinking about. They are "ecologically valid" in the sense that they present the kinds of information and requests for judgment that some people in our society confront every day. They are not the direct encounters with the physical or social worlds that we usually think of as the jumping-off point for scientific reasoning. The subjects address second-order realities—model ships, computer microworlds, data in a filing cabinet. They are, in effect, expected to look "through" them toward the real-world phenomena and subject the phenomena to scientific analysis.[1]

Educated adults in our society move back and forth between real things and rule-governed calculations about imaginary things so easily and comfortably that it takes some effort to realize that, inevitably, questions arise about how the subjects dealt with the media of the study and the fact that they were of human contrivance. The two physical problems were presented through dynamic simulations, while the two social problems were given by sets of static indicators. The two physical problems were reasonably "transparent" in that one could imagine a real-world transformation behind them; the simulations served as scaffolding for such acts of imagination. The two social problems were opaque to me. I tried to imagine the realities to which they alluded and conjured up some images of schoolchildren sitting at desks and working and some shadowy figures turning television sets on and off from time to time. Do subjects think differently about a perceivable physical transformation than they do about an unperceivable process indexed by categorical information? In this study, the social problems proved to be more difficult than the physical problems, and the authors discuss a number of possible reasons for this. It seemed to me that the two classes of problems held out to the subjects different sorts of indicators linked to very different kinds of realities. What is remarkable, really, is the human ability to translate questions about both those realities into the same kind of scientific reasoning exercise. But the subjects of the study may have had trouble staying carefully on the "surface" of the formal reasoning exercises—the "plane of the symbolic," Piaget once called it, where formal reasoning is possible—as students often will.

The subjects in the study knew that the problems presented to them were contrived by the researchers. The researchers designing the problems thought about which variables might or might not seem plausible to the subjects. Did the subjects confronting the problems, in turn, think about the researchers and "play" them—as a skilled college student "plays" the writer of the items on a multiple-choice test? It would have been worthwhile

[1] There is more to cognitive development than the solving of epistemological problems. The subjects addressing the physical problems were in the position of contemporary scientists examining natural phenomena through readings of their scientific instruments. The subjects addressing the social problems entered the universe of experience of middle management, complete with filing cabinet. Many of the scientific and professional jobs of a modern society are conducted by people who sit in windowless offices and use symbolic representations for sophisticated transactions with distal reality. Schools build the skills for this, and the capacity to operate in such second-order realities is, I believe, the intelligence that intelligence tests test for.

to ask the subjects about this. One might well find another (metasituational?) dimension of difference between the younger and the older subjects.

This work's contribution is at two levels—first as a substantive study saying something about how scientific reasoning develops and second as a methodologically innovative effort to bring idiographic and nomothetic approaches together in one research design. We look through a much larger window than is customary in studies of human learning and problem solving. Of particular importance is the joining of an idiographic and nomothetic approach: "In particular, the study of individual subjects is receiving increasing attention as an important and neglected method. As a research method, however, single-subject analysis most often is treated skeptically, and even dismissed, on the assumption that it is severely limited by its inability to provide evidence of the generality of the phenomena observed. Here, we undertake to illustrate how individual and group, as well as qualitative and quantitative, modes of analysis can be used in conjunction to provide an enriched understanding of developmental phenomena" (p. 6). The authors feel that the complex design of their study—enabling them to look at their individual subjects repeatedly, in the same and different situations, but at the same time enabling them to look at preadolescent versus adult subjects in the same situation—gives their study considerable power. Given the richness of the findings of the study, one cannot help but agree. The practical problems of subject recruitment did not allow for the perfect population-sampling scheme of inference that has been the ideal of group comparisons in nomothetic designs. We cannot be sure that our younger and older subjects were sampled from the same population, alike in all respects but for their ages. They came from the same neighborhood, to be sure, but we cannot know that the recruitment processes drew younger and older subjects out of the neighborhood in just the same way. Nor, since many of the older subjects were dealt with in Spanish while none of the younger ones was, can we say that the two age groups experienced the same treatment. Ultimately, the fundamental test for a study such as this (as it is for any statistical population-comparison study) is the question of whether its findings have clarity, coherence, and consistency with other findings. The rich body of data brought under discussion in this *Monograph* as well as the careful and detailed way in which this work is discussed in the context of other contemporary research strongly support the judgment that this is a meaningful analysis of the development of scientific reasoning.

The principal findings of the study give an interesting picture of the development of scientific reasoning in adolescence. There is fundamental variability of subjects' performances on problems such as this. The existence of this kind of human variability is usually underestimated in typical single-task, single-performance studies of problem solving, although we get a sense of it whenever we plot the scatter of any kind of reaction time or response time over trials. The logical metaphors and the computer metaphors that are at the heart of most theory-building exercises in psychology generally do not take this into account. People are unstable platforms for computation. We are subject to attention waves, rest-activity cycles, circadian rhythms, mood swings, and various other changes of state. Children do not always think in just the same way about problems from one time to the next.

There is a competition among strategies in the process of knowledge acquisition, right from the beginning. More adequate strategies compete with less adequate ones:

> Perhaps the most essential thing that our results indicate is what people definitely do *not* do in acquiring new knowledge, and that is simply to access and gradually accumulate evidence until they feel that they have enough to draw a conclusion. Instead, theoretical beliefs shape the evidence that is examined, the way in which that evidence is interpreted, and the conclusions that are drawn. The subjects . . . drew conclusions virtually from the outset, on the basis of minimal or no data, and then changed their minds repeatedly. . . . The challenge that the individual faces is one, then, not simply of correctly "reading" the data, but of coordinating theories and evidence. (p. 106)

The findings of the present study confirm the findings of a number of antecedent microgenetic studies of problem solving. All converge on the conclusion that knowledge change involves the competition of older, less adequate strategies with newer, more adequate ones. An important problem for cognitive change is the abandonment of an older strategy rather than the acquisition of the newer one, and, when it comes, such change is a matter of the redistribution of use of a number of strategies available to the subject. This is, it might be noted, a striking recapitulation in the data of cognitive psychology of the scheme of trial-and-error learning proposed by Edward L. Thorndike (1898) at the turn of this century.

Subjects of the study, the younger and the older, developed knowledge through coordinations of theory and evidence. They modified their theory-evidence coordinations using strategic, metastrategic, and metacognitive competencies. (The discussion of how they do this is elegant.) The performances of the two age groups were by no means cleanly separated. However, there were differences: "Our microgenetic . . . evidence for the progression described here stands as counterevidence to claims . . . that there is no evidence of fundamentally different forms of processing by immature, intuitive scientists and professional scientists" (p. 113). Adults and children differed in their possession of strategies, metacognitive knowledge, and metastrategic knowledge. The interesting question would be to try to detect, through the fundamental variability of the subjects' trial-by-trial processes, the interplay among the three kinds of knowledge elements and the way in which the emergence of one facilitates the emergence of another. The authors wrestle with this question but are not, as far as I can see, able to make headway with it. Probably, more sustained microgenetic studies, focusing on the interplay of the several cognitive elements, would give a richer picture of these changes.

In this very interesting and provocative study, we get a very good picture of one elaboration of Piagetian theory that is now taking place in this post-Piagetian era. Scientific reasoning develops in adolescence, as Piaget said, but not in the way he said. Instead of wide-sweeping structural changes in the logical engines available to the child, there are changes in cognitive elements that the child can call into play when confronted with a problematic situation. The changes are not wide sweeping. They are more local, particulate. Yet there is transfer. Developed in one context of use, the strategic, metastrategic, and metacognitive knowledges available to the child are brought into play in other contexts. The emergence of scientific reasoning depends, as Piaget observed, on the emergence of metacognitive cognition. But such cognition is not unique to older children, and the emergence of scientific reasoning depends on an orchestration of a number of cognitive elements that have to work together. Change, as it occurs, is by no means irreversible. It occurs by changes in the predispositions of various kinds of mental strategies available to the ever-varying child. While this is not consistent with the four-stage stereotype of Piaget's theory conventionally given in the textbooks, and while many details fall completely outside Piaget's scheme of adolescent thought development—in truth, he gave somewhat less attention to adolescence than he did to the earlier phases of children's development—it is a significant and not terribly inconsistent elaboration of the main body of his thinking about cognitive development.

## References

Kuhn, D. (1986). Education for thinking. *Teachers College Record,* **87,** 495–512.

Kuhn, D. (1989a). Children and adults as intuitive scientists. *Psychological Review,* **96,** 674–689.

Kuhn, D. (1989b). Making cognitive development research relevant to education. In W. Damon (Ed.), *Child development today and tomorrow.* San Francisco: Jossey-Bass.

Kuhn, D. (Ed.). (1990a). *Developmental perspectives on teaching and learning thinking skills* (Contributions to Human Development, Vol. **21**). Basel: Karger.

Kuhn, D. (1990b). Education for thinking: What can psychology contribute? In M. Schwebel, C. A. Maher, & N. S. Fagley (Eds.), *Promoting cognitive growth over the life span.* Hillsdale, NJ: Erlbaum.

Kuhn, D. (1992). Thinking as argument. *Harvard Educational Review,* **62,** 155–178.

Kuhn, D. (1993b). Connecting scientific and informal reasoning. *Merrill-Palmer Quarterly,* **39,** 74–103.

Kuhn, D. (1993b). Science as argument: Implications for teaching and learning scientific thinking. *Science Education,* **77,** 319–377.

Kuhn, D., Amsel, E., & O'Loughlin, M. (1988). *The development of scientific thinking skills.* San Diego: Academic.

Kuhn, D., Weinstock, M., & Flaton, R. (1994a). Historical reasoning as theory-evidence coordination. In M. Carretero & J. F. Voss (Eds.), *Cognitive and instructional processes in history and the social sciences.* Hillsdale, NJ: Erlbaum.

Kuhn, D., Weinstock, M., & Flaton, R. (1994b). How well do jurors reason? Competence dimensions of individual variation in a juror reasoning task. *Psychological Science,* **5,** 289–296.

Thorndike, E. L. (1898). Animal intelligence: An experimental study of the associative processes in animals. *Psychological Review, Monograph Supplements,* **2** (Serial No. 8).

# COMMENTARY

## SCIENTIFIC THINKING ABOUT SCIENTIFIC THINKING

*David Klahr and Sharon M. Carver*

Readers come to the Commentaries of these *Monographs* with three questions in mind. First, is the *Monograph* worth reading? Second, does it raise specific points that deserve further attention, emphasis, or criticism? Finally, are there broad issues raised by the *Monograph* that are sufficiently important to warrant further discussion, almost independent of the content of the *Monograph* itself? With respect to the present *Monograph,* the short answers to these questions are "yes," "yes," and "yes." The longer answers follow.

Kuhn, Garcia-Mila, Zohar, and Andersen address the question of how people generate evidence about multivariable causal systems and then form hypotheses about the relevant variables on the basis of that evidence. They investigated this issue in two broad domains (physical and social), using two groups of subjects (preadolescents and adults), and they focused on how, over the course of 10 weekly experimental sessions, subjects acquired not only domain-specific knowledge (e.g., the factors that make for fast cars or effective television commercials) but also domain-general strategies for making valid inferences from data. The design enabled Kuhn et al. to compare performance within and across domains and subject populations, and the analysis revealed important similarities and differences in the use of valid and invalid strategies that we will describe below.

Kuhn et al.'s ambitious and unprecedented undertaking embraces a densely interwoven tapestry of fundamental methodological issues and central topics within the area of cognitive development. The methodological issues include transfer of training, microgenetic analysis, and the relative merits of quantitative and qualitative analysis of children's behavior. The topical areas include scientific reasoning, strategy acquisition and choice, and metacognition.

In order to deal with this array of interconnected issues and topics, we have organized this Commentary into four sections. In the first, we provide a broad context for research on scientific discovery in which to situate the Kuhn et al. project, and we emphasize its considerable strengths. In the second section, we view the Kuhn et al. work from another perspective: as a transfer of training study. In the third, we raise both methodological and theoretical questions about the work. Finally, in the fourth section, we offer suggestions for addressing some of the questions stimulated by this remarkable investigation.

### *Investigating the Scientific Discovery Process*

The Kuhn et al. work is about many things, but it is, to our way of thinking, primarily an investigation of the scientific discovery process. The general paradigm used by psychologists who are interested in scientific reasoning is to present people with situations crafted to isolate one or more essential aspects of "real-world" science and to observe their problem-solving processes carefully. There are, of course, other ways to study scientific thinking, including historical analyses, retrospective reports, and "in vivo" studies of ongoing scientific work (Dunbar, 1994). However, the laboratory approach exemplified by the Kuhn et al. work has several important merits:

1. It allows the researcher great latitude in selecting the subject population under investigation.
2. It enables the researcher to exert substantial control over subjects' prior knowledge, through the type of selection mentioned above and through various levels of background training in the domain under investigation.
3. It facilitates the observation of the dynamic course of scientific discovery in great detail and the corresponding use of a variety of assessment methodologies.
4. It allows control over the "state of nature," that is, the thing to be discovered by the subjects. Such studies have presented subjects with a variety of things to be discovered, including (*a*) an arbitrary rule that the experimenter has in mind (Gorman, 1992; Wason, 1960), (*b*) a computer microworld that embodies some realistic causal factors and some arbitrary ones (such as the race cars microworld developed by Schauble, 1990, and used by Kuhn et al.), (*c*) the causal factors in a real physical domain, such as the boat task used by Kuhn et al. (adapted from a task created by Schauble, Klopfer, & Raghavan, 1991) or the investigation of sinking rates of objects dropped in water (Penner &

Klahr, in press), (*d*) the physics of a complex artificial universe (Mynatt, Doherty, & Tweney, 1977), and (*e*) a computer microworld designed to capture the essential features of a historical discovery (e.g., Dunbar's, 1993, microworld in which subjects attempted to [re]discover the mechanisms of genetic inhibition).

5. Perhaps the most valuable characteristic of laboratory studies of scientific reasoning is that they included a well-documented record of the unsuccessful, as well as the successful, discoverers. Because there is a scant historical or biographical record of the myriad failures of discovery, historical approaches to the psychology of scientific discovery can catalog only sufficient causes for discovery. They cannot tell us anything about necessary causes. Laboratory studies allow us to look at both successful and unsuccessful subjects and enable us to determine what distinguishes them.

The challenge posed by investigating the psychology of scientific discovery in "real time" is to find a way to evoke the cognitive processes inherent in scientific discovery while maintaining the experimental rigor that supports sound inferences about human cognition. Despite the difficulty of this task, the Kuhn et al. project is unusually successful in using a set of domains having all the above characteristics. In the next section, we place their work in the context of other attempts to study various aspects of scientific thinking.

### *Laboratory Investigations of the Cognitive Psychology of Science*

Laboratory investigations of scientific reasoning can be classified along two dimensions: one representing the degree of domain specificity or domain generality and the other representing the type of processes involved. Table 1 depicts this characterization of the field. The two rows correspond to the difference between domain-general knowledge and domain-specific knowledge, and the three columns correspond to the major components of the overall discovery process: searching a space of hypotheses, searching a

TABLE 1

TYPES OF FOCI IN PSYCHOLOGICAL STUDIES OF SCIENTIFIC REASONING PROCESSES

| | Hypothesis Space Search | Experiment Space Search | Evidence Evaluation |
|---|---|---|---|
| Domain-specific knowledge and strong methods ................ | A | B | C |
| Domain-general knowledge and weak methods ................. | D | E | F |

SOURCE.—Klahr (1994).

space of experiments, and evaluating evidence. Psychologists' attempts to disentangle the relative influence of general versus specific knowledge have produced two distinct literatures: one on domain-specific knowledge and "strong methods" and the other on domain-general reasoning processes and "weak methods." This distinction corresponds to the two rows in Table 1.

The three columns in Table 1 reflect a view of scientific discovery as a type of problem-solving process involving search in a problem space (Newell & Simon, 1972). In the case of scientific discovery, there are two primary spaces to be searched: a space of hypotheses and a space of experiments. These spaces are sufficiently different that they require different representations, different operators for moving about in the space, and different criteria for what constitutes progress in the space. Without getting into detail here (see Klahr & Dunbar, 1988), we can convey the importance of the distinction between searching the hypothesis space and searching the experiment space by noting that, in most of the natural sciences, the difference between experimental work and theoretical work is so great as to have individuals who claim to be experts in one but not the other aspect of their discipline.

It is clear that the problems to be solved in each space are different, even though they have obvious and necessary mutual influences. Thus, in our characterization of research on scientific discovery, we emphasize three major interdependent processes: hypothesis space search, experiment space search, and evidence evaluation. In searching the hypothesis space, the initial state consists of some knowledge about a domain, and the goal state is a hypothesis that can account for some or all of that knowledge. When one or more hypotheses are active, it is not immediately obvious what constitutes a "good" experiment. In constructing experiments, subjects are faced with a problem-solving task paralleling their search for hypotheses. That is, they must search in the experiment space for an informative experiment.

The third process—evidence evaluation—involves a comparison of the predictions derived from the current hypothesis with the results obtained from experimentation. In the studies reported in this *Monograph,* the considerable emphasis on strategies for valid inferences deals mainly with this phase of the process.

During the course of scientific discovery, the various cells in Table 1 are traversed repeatedly. However, it is very difficult to study thinking processes that involve all of them simultaneously. Consequently, the early research in the field started with investigations designed to constrain the topic of interest to just one or two cells. As the field has matured, more complex contexts involving multiple cells have been used. We can best illustrate this with a few examples of investigations that involve various cells from Table 1.

*Cell A.*—Investigations falling into this cell are exemplified by McCloskey's (1983) well-known investigation of people's naive theories of motion. In this kind of study, subjects are asked about their knowledge about a specific domain, but they do not run experiments, and they do not evaluate evidence.

*Cell B.*—In some investigations (e.g., Tschirgi, 1980), subjects are asked to decide which of a set of prespecified experiments will demonstrate the correctness of a prespecified hypothesis. There is no search for hypotheses, and the experiment space search is limited to choosing among alternative experiments.

*Cells D, E, and F.*—Bruner, Goodnow, and Austin (1956) created their classic concept-learning task in order to better understand people's appreciation of the logic of experimentation and their strategies for discovering regularities. Their subjects had to generate hypotheses, choose among "experiments" (i.e., select different cards that displayed specific combinations of attributes), and evaluate the evidence provided by the yes/no feedback that they received. Because the task is abstract and arbitrary, none of the domain-specific cells are involved. Another venerable task that spans cells D, E, and F is Wason's (1960) 2-4-6 task.

*Cell E.*—Studies of people's ability to design factorial experiments (e.g., Case, 1974; Siegler & Liebert, 1975) focus almost entirely on effective search of the experiment space. Domain knowledge is minimized, as are hypothesis space search and evidence evaluation.

*Cells C and F.*—Studies in this category focus on people's ability to decide which of several hypotheses is supported by evidence. Typically, such studies present tables of covariation data and ask subjects to decide which of several hypotheses is supported or refuted by the data. In some cases, the factors are abstract and arbitrary (e.g., Shaklee & Paszek, 1985)—in which case we classify the studies in Cell F—and in others they refer to real-world factors (e.g., plant growth in the context of different amounts of sunlight and water; Bullock & Ziegler, in press). In such cases, subjects have to coordinate their prior domain knowledge with the covariation data in the tables (e.g., Ruffman, Perner, Olson, & Doherty, 1993).

### *Integrative Investigations of Scientific Reasoning*

Research focusing on either domain-specific or domain-general knowledge has yielded much useful information about scientific discovery. However, such efforts are, perforce, unable to assess the interaction between the two types of knowledge. Similarly, the isolation of hypothesis search, experimentation strategies, and evidence evaluation begs some fundamental questions. How are the three main processes integrated? How do they mutually influence one another?

Although many investigations focus on one or two of the cells depicted in Table 1, few studies attempt to traverse the entire matrix. Such investigations are necessary to really understand scientific reasoning because in "real science" both domain-specific knowledge and domain-general heuristics guide scientists in designing experiments and evaluating their outcomes. More informative are tasks requiring coordinated search in *both* the experiment space and the hypothesis space as well as the evaluation of evidence produced by subject-generated experiments.

Kuhn and her colleagues have pioneered this kind of research (cf. Kuhn, 1989; Kuhn, Amsel, & O'Loughlin, 1988; Kuhn, Schauble, & Garcia-Mila, 1992; Schauble, 1990; Schauble, Glaser, Raghavan, & Reiner, 1991), and the present *Monograph* represents yet another valuable extension of the approach. Although others have created similar "discovery contexts" in which to investigate the development of scientific reasoning processes (Dunbar, 1993; Klahr & Dunbar, 1988; Klahr, Fay, & Dunbar, 1993), only Kuhn and her colleagues have combined this integrated approach to scientific discovery with a microgenetic approach. Moreover, with respect to domain-specific reasoning, the Kuhn et al. work represents the first such study that simultaneously utilizes two distinct types of domains and examines the mutual influence of reasoning in one domain on reasoning in the other. One can depict the Kuhn et al. study as a series of layers of 2 × 3 tables, as shown in Figure 1. Each layer represents a single session in which all the cells are traversed, and the series of layers represent the time course of densely connected repeated assessments of how subjects traverse these spaces.

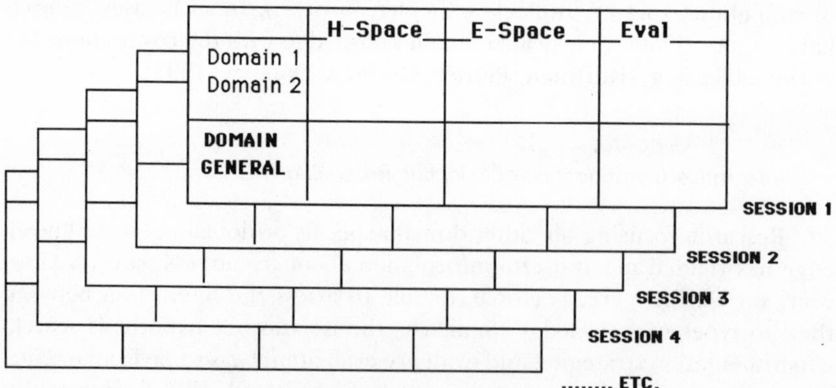


FIG. 1.—Microgenetic study of scientific reasoning

### Transfer of Training

Another unique and valuable feature of this work is the way in which it focuses on the temporal course of *both* of the knowledge types depicted in Figure 1: knowledge about the specific domain (e.g., boats, school achievement) and domain-general knowledge about scientific reasoning (e.g., valid inclusion). It is these domain-general processes that Kuhn et al. emphasize in their title: *Strategies of Knowledge Acquisition*. Moreover, Kuhn et al.'s ingenious design allows them to assess the extent to which the knowledge acquisition strategies acquired in one domain transfer to another domain. In other words, Kuhn et al. have a direct measure of how domain general such skills really are.

Kuhn et al. comment on the mixed picture provided by earlier investigations of transfer, and they ask, "Why did our subjects show transfer of newly developing cognitive strategies when transfer so often fails to occur in both children and adults?" (p. 100). We find this question particularly intriguing because we have previously described what we believe to be sufficient conditions for transfer: "*If* the domain is properly analyzed, *if* instruction is based on the formal analysis, and *if* what is learned in the base domain and what is transferred to more remote domains are also grounded in the formal analysis, *then* a powerful idea . . . can be taught and can have an impact on general problem-solving capacities" (Klahr & Carver, 1988, pp. 364–364).

Given the design and results of the present study, it appears that our conditions are, at best, a statement of sufficiency rather than necessity, for the procedure used by Kuhn et al. seems to honor none of our conditions for transfer. In fact, not only is transfer surprising, but so is learning, because the experimenter provides the subjects with no feedback about the efficacy of the inference strategies currently being used to evaluate experimental outcomes. Although the experiments that subjects run give them a substantial amount of feedback about the domain under investigations, there is *no* direct feedback about the next level of knowledge acquisition—the inferencing strategies—yet this is what subjects learned, and this is what transferred from one context to the next.

On the other hand, a careful look at the Kuhn et al. procedure reveals that the kind of carefully elaborated goal structure that we include in our sufficiency list *is* inherent in the sequence of questions and probes that precede and follow each of the subject's experiments. Although subjects do not get feedback in the traditional sense, they do receive a kind of Socratic dialogue as they are walked through the goal structure that underlies valid inferencing and the coordination of theory and evidence. It is quite likely that subjects have never been presented with such a highly structured sequence of probes about how and why they examined specific pieces of evidence or drew specific conclusions from that evidence. For this reason, the Kuhn et al. study should be viewed not only as a study of transfer but also as a study of transfer of *training* (and a successful one at that!).

### *Theoretical and Methodological Questions*

In addition to the substantial strengths listed thus far, the *Monograph* raises important points that warrant further attention, and we address several of them in this section. We start with the observation that only a limited subset of the many forms of knowledge acquisition were actually studied here: selection of instances and the formation of valid inferences from patterns of covariation and noncovariation. But how much of people's knowledge is acquired through the coordination of theory and evidence? Although attempts to answer this question precisely may founder on the problem of quantification of "amount" of knowledge, it seems to us that very little of one's overall knowledge base comes from experimentation. Instead, most of it comes from generalizations over particular instances, or from reading, or from direct instruction from parents and teachers. It seems that little of what we know about what factors contribute to fast cars or fast boats comes from running experiments (confounded or not) in those domains. Moreover, it is even less likely that we acquire knowledge via experimentation in the social domain than it is in the physical domain. Thus, we claim that the work reported here is not so much about "knowledge acquisition" as it is about the narrower—but still important—context of scientific reasoning.

#### *Strategies and Metacognition*

Our second question is also related to another key term in the title of this *Monograph—strategies.* Over the past decade or so, the term *strategy* has undergone a transformation from its original use in game theory—that is, a deliberate, rational, intentional scheme to achieve an end—to a more amorphous notion describing any set of organized processes or rules, intentional or not, explicit or not. In its present usage, exemplified here and also by Siegler's focus on "strategy choice" (Siegler & Shipley, 1995), one could easily replace *strategy* with the generic term *process.* Indeed, we question the extent to which it is productive to label these and other knowledge acquisition processes as strategies. Would it make sense to call associative learning, learning from instruction, or learning from reading *strategies*?

This transformation of *strategy* from a well-defined to a generic notion results in even more ambiguity when one discusses *metastrategic* issues, as do Kuhn et al. in their characterization of subjects using strategies "selectively and variably." This implies some higher-level agent that controls the selection and variation process and justifies the various levels of metacognition that Kuhn et al. invoke. The problem with this conception is that those processes of strategy selection and strategy variation are not explained at all. This lack of specification is not an uncommon result of invoking metacognitive processes. As Siegler & Shipley (1995) note:

> Such metacognitive models are useful for conveying hypotheses about relations among different types of knowledge and for pointing to one way in which intelligent strategy choices can be generated. However, they also have a number of weaknesses. . . . As statements of theory, they generally have been vague regarding the mechanisms that produce the phenomena of interest. Do people make explicit judgments about their intellectual capacities, available strategies, and task demands every time they face a task they could perform in multiple ways? If not, how do they decide when to do so? Do they consider every strategy they could use on the task, or only some of them? If only some, how do they decide which ones? How do people know what their cognitive capacity will be on a novel task or what strategies they could apply to it? The apparent simplicity of metacognitive models masks a world of complexity. (p. 41)

### *Microgenetic Method*

Kuhn and her colleagues represent one of the primary influences on the current reemergence of microgenetic methods, and the current *Monograph* is yet another valuable example of the approach. But there are some important differences between the way that Kuhn et al. use the method and the way it is characterized by some of its other advocates (Siegler & Crowley, 1991). Kuhn et al. argue that a primary goal of the microgenetic method is "to accelerate the change process by providing a subject with frequent opportunities over a period of weeks or months to engage the particular cognitive strategies that are the object of investigation" (p. 8). The idea is to run a sort of cognitive "summer camp" that includes extensive exercise of the cognitive skill to be acquired. Siegler and Crowley, on the other hand, do not view the method itself as the necessary cause for the acceleration. Instead, they propose conducting a preliminary analysis of the natural developmental course in a domain and then ensuring that "observations span the entire period from the beginning of the change to the time at which it reaches a relatively stable state" (Siegler & Crowley, 1991, p. 606). For them, the repeated exposures are not so much a way of stimulating or prodding the change process as they are a procedure for generating a high "sampling rate" so that the change process can be observed in detail.

Another important distinction—albeit not a disagreement—is Siegler and Crowley's focus on cognitive skills that just about everyone acquires in the natural course of development (such as quantity conservation or the min method for single-digit addition). This focus leads Siegler and Crowley to associate with the microgenetic method the determination of a critical window of opportunity during which to observe the changes of interest. In contrast, Kuhn et al. have focused on a skill that few people master without formal training (valid inferences from empirical data). Thus, rather than seek a critical period in which to locate their observations, they made the strategic bet that both adolescents and adults would start at similar levels of knowledge. As their results show, this was indeed the case. Not only did both groups start at similar levels, but both also demonstrated significant changes in their knowledge level over the course of the microgenetic observations.

### *On the Logic of Confirmation and Disconfirmation*

The conceptual core of this *Monograph* is Kuhn et al.'s analysis of "inductive causal and noncausal inference." Given the fundamental importance of the strategies that support such inferences, it is surprising that Kuhn et al. make no contact with the extensive literature on "confirmation bias" or with Klayman and Ha's (1987) elegant analysis of the role of confirmation and disconfirmation strategies in rule discovery tasks. Although Klayman and Ha focus on the classic 2-4-6 rule discovery task, in which subjects have to discover a rule that is being used to classify triples of integers (Wason, 1960), their analysis has implications for the work reported here.

Kuhn et al. note that a single instance in which a feature and an outcome co-occur can lead, at best, to what they call a "co-occurrence false inclusion inference" (p. 19). However, if subjects construe their task as a rule discovery task, then they may establish goals to create "experiments" that are (or are not) "instances" of, for example, the "fast rule." To the extent that subjects adopt this rule discovery stance, the literature on confirmation bias is highly relevant to the current *Monograph.* Nearly all previous investigations of the Wason task (e.g., Gorman, 1986, 1989; Wason, 1960) concluded that subjects approach rule discovery tasks with a strong "confirmation bias": a desire to select instances that confirm ("+Htests") rather disconfirm ("−Htests") the current hypothesis. In other words, "people tend to test hypotheses by looking at instances where the target property is hypothesized to be present" (Klayman & Ha, 1987, p. 225).

However, as Klayman and Ha note, there is no logical basis for interpreting +Htests as attempts to confirm or −Htests as attempts to disconfirm. Depending on the relation between the hypothesized rule and the true rule, both +Htests and −Htests can provide either conclusive falsification or ambiguous verification of the current hypothesis. Conclusive falsification occurs when a +Htest receives "no" feedback (e.g., when a subject who believes that big motors make for fast cars creates a car with a big motor that runs slowly) or when a −Htest receives "yes" feedback (e.g., when a subject who believes that big motors make for fast cars creates a car with a small motor that runs fast). Ambiguous verification occurs when a +Htest receives "yes" feedback (the big motor does produce a fast car) or when a −Htest receives "no" feedback (the small motor does produce a slow car). The conclusiveness or ambiguity of these outcomes derives from the standard falsificationist arguments (Popper, 1959). Thus, +Htesting "does not necessarily contradict the goal of seeking falsification" (Klayman & Ha, 1987, p. 225). In the general scheme of things, most factors are noncausal rather than causal. Consequently, from an efficiency point of view, one should focus on the plausibly causal factors and run +Htests on them while deferring consideration of the potentially infinite number of noncausal factors until it becomes necessary to explore further.

Further complicating the labeling of subjects' strategies as *valid* or *invalid* is the fact that, for those cases in which subjects have very strong beliefs about the irrelevance of certain factors, it is inappropriate to fault them for running what an omniscient observer would characterize as confounded experiments. As experimenters, we routinely fail to control all possible confounds. For example, in the current *Monograph,* we can be fairly sure that the proportion of parents and married subjects was greater in the adult sample than in the adolescent sample or that the number of years since the last formal schooling was greater for the adults than for the adolescents. Thus, all comparisons between adults and children are confounded by these factors, yet it would be foolish to call any conclusions about adult-child differences here *false inclusions* or *false exclusions* because these covariates were not controlled.

### *The Equivalence of Experimentation in Social and Physical Domains*

One of the most interesting features of the Kuhn et al. study is the way in which it contrasts performance not only between different problems within a domain (i.e., boats vs. cars) but also between the social and the physical domains. In order to accomplish this, Kuhn et al. faced a formidable challenge in the creation of materials and procedures that would keep all the important aspects of "running experiments" equivalent in both domains. Kuhn et al.'s inventive solution to this problem was to create a set of records that have to be examined by subjects, thereby making it feasible to run "experiments" in the social domain. However, the solution is not entirely satisfactory because many potentially important differences between the two domains—other than the domain as such—remain.

One difference is that, in the physical domain, the causal mechanisms that determine the outcome operate only *after* subjects have selected a set of features, whereas, in the social domain, the features and their effects have been determined *prior* to the selection of the card that shows what those effects were. Although the two domains have identical causal structures, they differ with respect to this potentially important aspect. Recent emphasis on the importance of future-oriented thinking (Haith, Pennington, & Benson, 1994) suggests that this is not a trivial difference, yet all social-physical comparisons are compromised by this confound. The confound could have been eliminated if, in the physical domain, the experimental results were all precomputed and stored in the same kind of card catalog as was used in the social domain.

Furthermore, we would expect that, for most subjects, the process of making inferences (valid or not) on the basis of selected sets of instances is a rare activity in the social domain, although it may be a typical "science class" type of activity. In fact, subjects are likely to have strong personal opinions about the social domains, with a fair amount of associated affect, which is unlikely in the physical domain.

Another potentially important difference between the physical and the social domains is that, although in the physical domain categorical outcomes were used, it was clear to the subject that they were categorizations of things that had an underlying continuum on a ratio scale. In the social domain, categorical labels do not have clear correspondence to a scale. In other words, one distance can be twice as far as another in the race car domain, but, in the social domain, such quantification is impossible.

Finally, in at least one of the physical domains but none of the social domains, subjects understand that the outcomes that they see are not "rigged" by the experimenter. Instead, the laws of physics determine the outcomes. In the social domain, it is never clear the extent to which subjects really believe that the outcomes on the cards realistically portray the social world from which their initial beliefs derive.

All these differences between the social and the physical domains make the Kuhn et al. comparisons between them vulnerable to the very criticism of confounded experimentation and false inclusion that is the subject of investigation in this *Monograph.* (We are aware that all investigations of scientific reasoning are prey to this kind of reflexive criticism, but it seems so serious in this instance as to be unavoidable.)

### *Levels of Analysis in Microgenetic Research*

Kuhn et al. note that "qualitative case study analysis deserves more respect and use than it receives from most developmental psychologists." They continue, "Qualitative and quantitative analysis can be used in complementary ways that enhance understanding beyond what would be achieved by either method alone" (p. 000). Although we fully concur with the general claim, we believe that Kuhn et al.'s use of both types of analysis could have been more informative. On the one hand, their quantitative analyses are presented at very high levels of aggregation, with no quantitative information about how individual subjects acquired domain knowledge or how they utilized valid and invalid inclusion and exclusion strategies. For example, all the tables comparing subject's initial and final strategies fail to indicate the extent to which *individual* subjects changed or retained their initial domain theories. On the other hand, Kuhn et al.'s "qualitative analyses" fail to go beyond an informal narrative description of the experience of individual subjects. Some important information is not provided: what in Arnie's background might account for his outstanding performance? When and why did individual subjects use their notebooks in evaluating their experimental outcomes? In addition to providing more of this kind of information, one can perform a more systematic analysis of verbal protocols, seeking characteristic patterns of domain knowledge and inferencing strategies and quantifying aspects of individual protocols by segmenting the protocols into episodes that are, in turn, subject to quantitative analyses (cf. Ericsson & Simon, 1984).

### *Suggestions for Future Studies*

Kuhn et al. characterize their work as "bridge building" (p. 118). As inhabitants of a region with more than 500 bridges (White & von Bernewitz, 1928), we fully appreciate their value. We find, however, that, like many of those in and around Pittsburgh, some of the bridges suggested in this *Monograph* are in need of some skeptical examination. Kuhn et al. claim that their "most basic and possibly single most important result" is that "exercise of reasoning strategies can be a sufficient condition to effect their change" and that, "if reasoning is practiced, consistency in application of sound strategies is likely to improve" (p. 119). Although this view is consistent with much of the rhetoric surrounding radical constructivist approaches to learning, we find two problems with it. First, in its starkest form, the claim is simply not supported by the results reported in this *Monograph.* Second, it leaves the process of knowledge acquisition and strategy change unexplained.

The Kuhn et al. claims quoted suggest that the "exercise" that leads to learning is entirely learner directed. However, as we noted earlier, a crucial feature of their methodology was the use of a systematic set of probes that, in effect, indicated to subjects an underlying goal structure for searching the experiment space and the hypothesis space and for making valid inferences when evaluating evidence. We believe that, absent this highly structured and often-repeated set of questions, the undirected "exercise of reasoning strategies" would lead to little learning. In fact, although Kuhn et al. allude to the "transfer on trial" literature, careful examination of that literature shows that the few successful cases of transfer are precisely those in which either the underlying goal structure of the domain or systematic feedback about the outcome of the strategy use, or both, is provided to subjects. Moreover, there are existing accounts of learning that explain why and how these conditions promote learning and transfer (Anderson, 1993; Anderson, Reder, & Simon, 1995; Singley & Anderson, 1989). Given the importance that Kuhn et al. attribute to efficacy of strategic "exercise," it would be informative to replicate this type of study with and without the explicit probes that we claim are providing so much of the guidance for strategy change.

Finally, we suggest that, in future studies of this type, both the "qualitative" and the "quantitative" analyses be designed to dig deeper and probe further. To use another local metaphor, it strikes us that the data collected for this *Monograph* represent a potentially rich lode, but one that has only been strip-mined rather than deep mined.

### *References*


Anderson, J. R. (1993). *Rules of the mind.* Hillsdale, NJ: Erlbaum.

Anderson, J. R., Reder, L. M., & Simon, H. A. (1995). *Applications and misapplications of cognitive psychology to mathematics education.* Unpublished manuscript, Carnegie Mellon University.

Bruner, J. S., Goodnow, J. J., & Austin, G. A. (1956). *A study of thinking.* New York: Science Editions.

Bullock, M., & Ziegler, A. (in press). Scientific reasoning: Developmental and individual differences. In F. Weinert & W. Schneider (Eds.), *Individual development from 3 to 12: Findings from the Munich Longitudinal Study.* New York: Cambridge University Press.

Case, R. (1974). Structures and strictures: Some functional limitations on the course of cognitive growth. *Cognitive Psychology,* **6,** 544–573.

Dunbar, K. (1993). Concept discovery in a scientific domain. *Cognitive Science,* **17,** 397–434.

Dunbar, K. (1994). How scientists really reason: Scientific reasoning in real-world laboratories. In R. J. Sternberg & J. Davidson (Eds.), *Mechanisms of insight.* Cambridge, MA: MIT Press.

Ericsson, A., & Simon, H. A. (1984). *Protocol analysis: Verbal reports as data.* Cambridge, MA: MIT Press.

Gorman, M. E. (1986). How the possibility of error affects falsification on a task that models scientific problem solving. *British Journal of Psychology,* **77,** 85–96.

Gorman, M. E. (1989). Error, falsification and scientific inference: An experimental investigation. *Quarterly Journal of Experimental Psychology,* **41A**(2), 385–412.

Gorman, M. E. (1992). *Simulating science: Heuristics, mental models, and technoscientific thinking.* Bloomington: Indiana University Press.

Haith, M., Pennington, B., & Benson, J. (Eds.). (1994). *The development of future-oriented processes.* Chicago: University of Chicago Press.

Klahr, D. (1994). Searching for cognition in cognitive models of science. *Psycoloquy* **5**(94), scientific-cognition.12.klahr.

Klahr, D., & Carver, S. M. (1988). Cognitive objectives in a LOGO debugging curriculum: Instruction, learning, and transfer. *Cognitive Psychology,* **20,** 362–404.

Klahr, D., & Dunbar, K. (1988). Dual space search during scientific reasoning. *Cognitive Science,* **12**(1), 1–55.

Klahr, D., Fay, A. L., & Dunbar, K. (1993). Heuristics for scientific experimentation: A developmental study. *Cognitive Psychology,* **25**(1), 111–146.

Klayman, J., & Ha, Y. (1987). Confirmation, disconfirmation and information in hypothesis testing. *Psychological Review,* **94,** 211–228.

Kuhn, D. (1989). Children and adults as intuitive scientists. *Psychological Review,* **96,** 674–689.

Kuhn, D., Amsel, E., & O'Loughlin, M. (1988). *The development of scientific reasoning skills.* Orlando, FL: Academic.

Kuhn, D., Schauble, L., & Garcia-Mila, M. (1992). Cross-domain development of scientific reasoning. *Cognition and Instruction,* **9,** 285–327.

McCloskey, M. (1983). Naive theories of motion. In D. Gentner & A. L. Stevens (Eds.), *Mental models.* Hillsdale, NJ: Erlbaum.

Mynatt, C. R., Doherty, M. E., & Tweney, R. D. (1977). Confirmation bias in a simulated research environment: An experimental study of scientific inference. *Quarterly Journal of Experimental Psychology,* **29,** 85–95.

Newell, A., & Simon, H. A. (1972). *Human problem solving.* Englewood Cliffs, NJ: Prentice-Hall.

Penner, D., & Klahr, D. (1995). *The interaction of domain-specific knowledge and domain-general discovery strategies: A study with sinking objects.* Working paper.

Popper, K. R. (1959). *The logic of scientific discovery.* London: Hutchinson.

Ruffman, T., Perner, J., Olson, D. R., & Doherty, M. (1993). Reflecting on scientific thinking: Children's understanding of the hypothesis-evidence relation. *Child Development,* **64,** 1617–1636.

Schauble, L. (1990). Belief revision in children: The role of prior knowledge and strategies for generating evidence. *Journal of Experimental Child Psychology,* **49,** 31–57.

Schauble, L., Glaser, R., Raghavan, K., & Reiner, M. (1991). Causal models and experimentation strategies in scientific reasoning. *Journal of the Learning Sciences,* **1,** 201–238.

Schauble, L., Klopfer, L. E., & Raghavan, K. (1991). Students' transition from an engineering model to a science model of experimentation. *Journal of Research in Science Teaching,* **28,** 859–882.

Shaklee, H., & Paszek, D. (1985). Covariation judgment: Systematic rule use in middle childhood. *Child Development,* **56,** 1229–1240.

Siegler, R. S., & Crowley, K. (1991). The microgenetic method: A direct means for studying cognitive development. *American Psychologist,* **46,** 606–620.

Siegler, R. S., & Liebert, R. M. (1975). Acquisition of formal scientific reasoning by 10- and 13-year-olds: Designing a factorial experiment. *Developmental Psychology,* **10,** 401–402.

Siegler, R. S., & Shipley, C. (1995). Variation, selection, and cognitive change. In G. Halford & T. Simon (Eds.), *Developing cognitive competence: New approaches to process modeling.* Hillsdale, NJ: Erlbaum.

Singley, K., & Anderson, J. R. (1989). *The transfer of cognitive skills.* Cambridge, MA: Harvard University Press.

Tschirgi, J. E. (1980). Sensible reasoning: A hypothesis about hypotheses. *Child Development,* **51,** 1–10.

Wason, P. C. (1960). On the failure to eliminate hypotheses in a conceptual task. *Quarterly Journal of Experimental Psychology,* **12,** 129–140.

White, J., & von Bernewitz, M. W. (1928). *The bridges of Pittsburgh.* Pittsburgh: Carmer.

# REPLY

## SCIENTIFIC THINKING AND KNOWLEDGE ACQUISITION

*Deanna Kuhn*

My colleagues and I are grateful to Sheldon White and to David Klahr and Sharon Carver for their thoughtful reactions to our work. They offer a wide-ranging set of comments that touch on many topics, not all of which I will attempt to take up here. I would like to comment briefly on several points, but I want to focus first on the most fundamental question to be raised—namely, what is this *Monograph* about?

Both sets of commentators, quite reasonably, focus on our work as a study of scientific reasoning, which Klahr and Carver categorize as a subtopic within the broader topic of knowledge acquisition. Accepting this categorization, we might then ask why one would want to study scientific reasoning and its development. I recall debating this question with David Klahr at a conference a few years ago. The evening entertainment had begun, and we struggled to hear one another over the adjacent band music, so I cannot be certain that I am characterizing David's position entirely accurately. But the position I believe he took is that he and his colleagues have studied the development of scientific reasoning for much the same reason that Piaget undertook his genetic studies—to better understand this form of thought in its mature form (in this case, as practiced by professional scientists).

My own interest in scientific reasoning has been motivated by a different question—namely, what is the role of scientific thinking in thinking more broadly? The present *Monograph,* I hope, makes the contribution of highlighting the role and value of what we call scientific thinking in contexts other than scientific ones. Scientific thinking, which has intended to stand alone as a topic of scientific investigation, needs to be linked to inductive inference—regarded as a core knowledge acquisition process by cognitive psychologists (Holland, Holyoak, Nisbett, & Thagard, 1986), as we note in the text—and to assume the place it deserves as a vital mechanism of knowledge acquisition for all individuals.

Klahr and Carver assert that only a small portion of knowledge acquisition occurs through formal scientific experimentation, and, as long as we regard scientific thinking in this narrow sense, they are of course right. As developmental psychologists, we have to a large extent studied knowledge acquisition as an effortless, unconscious process that brings young children into alignment with their cultures. Or, as educational psychologists, we study it as the effortful and conscious mastery of particular bodies of knowledge, usually in academic contexts. The contribution we hope to have made to the study of knowledge acquisition is the idea that the strategies examined in this *Monograph*—notably, the more competent inference strategies on which we focus—are critical tools that, with development, may be added to an individual's knowledge acquisition capabilities. The fact that they are not universally mastered only adds to their significance. Freedom to choose the data to be examined is not the essential characteristic that gives these strategies their power and scope; they are even more important, I would claim, in the "natural experiment" context of inductive inference, precisely because of their vast range of application. What is developmentally significant about these strategies, as we emphasize in the text, is the control over one's own thought that they afford. They provide us the metaknowledge of what we do not know (what we cannot conclude as well as what we can) and, most important, of *how* we know what we do.

This brings us to the topic of "meta-" factors as critical components of cognition and cognitive development. We agree with Klahr and Carver that we have a long way to go in explaining how a metastrategic component functions to select strategies from a repertory, and we accept White's judgment that we have not made great headway in specifying how the three components—strategic, metastrategic, and metacognitive—interact to effect development. There is indeed a "world of complexity," as Klahr and Carver note, underlying a multicomponent model of this sort, and, in order to address it, we must sacrifice, or at least postpone, the very precise modeling that information-processing theorists favor.

The reason we should make this sacrifice, I believe, is that, without a model that includes such "meta-" components, we are further away from what it is that needs to be explained. People do operate on and exercise a degree of control over their thought processes. As White notes, although a connection can be made between metacognition and Piaget's formal operations, metacognitive processes are not unique to a particular developmental stage but rather a constant aspect of the mechanism that propels development. Once such processes are acknowledged, we need to develop a vocabulary to talk about and examine them—one that will likely come to be more extensive and differentiated than the simple tripartite one that we have proposed—just as the more generic use of the term *strategy* arguably arose because a term was needed to refer to actor-initiated mental actions, a need that the earlier generic term *response* did not fill.

The experience of collecting the data reported in this *Monograph* did leave us with a very concrete and vivid sense of that which needs to be explained—and how different it is from the earlier *explanandum* that preoccupied developmental psychologists, that of how the transition from one stable stage to another is achieved. After a period of time working with a subject, we came to know the repertory of different inferences that this subject was likely to use. Each of us took part in different portions of the data collection, and we each found it an experience of continuing amazement—even awesome and humbling mystery—to sit next to a subject as he or she accessed the same or a similar piece of data as had been accessed numerous times before and pondered it while we silently waited, our knowing that what was to come out of the subject's mouth could equally well be an impeccable scientific inference or a patently transparent fallacy. And we were unable to predict which it was going to be. Unless we are satisfied with a simple associative strength model, it is difficult to see how this mystery can be addressed without invoking a model that includes "meta-" components.

Metastrategic and metacognitive factors are also in large part the ones that differentiated our own scientific reasoning from that of our subjects. We understand the potential complications signified by the fact that many of our older subjects were married and none of our younger ones were, as Klahr and Carver note, or that older subjects may have had a more sophisticated understanding of the research context than younger ones, as White notes, and we know the ways in which such complications jeopardize our inferences. We make judgments about such issues—judgments that, for example, lead us to be more concerned about the latter difference than the former one—and we proceed accordingly. As researchers, we focus our attention on theoretically plausible variables for much the same reasons our subjects do—because they are more interesting "better bets" than variables we believe to be noncausal. But, unlike so many of our subjects, we know what we don't know, and we constrain our inferences accordingly, rather than asserting with certainty, for example, as our subjects so often did, not just that a particular factor makes no difference but that the data show that this is so (data that in many cases, recall, left the factor entirely unexamined).

One set of possibly confounding factors to which we gave considerable thought was the set of largely unavoidable procedural differences between the physical and the social task conditions. We do not claim to have pinpointed the essential difference between logical and social cognition. This is a question that continues to preoccupy the field, as the recent flurry of theory-of-mind research attests. In White's words, the contrast we constructed is between "a perceivable physical transformation" and "an unperceivable process indexed by categorical information" (p. 132). But how is this distinction itself to be categorized? The dividing line between procedural and essential difference is not clear-cut. Physical events are for the most part directly observable, whereas social phenomena always involve some degree of inference, that is, categorization.

Our results document that there does indeed exist a performance difference (across physical and social domains) to be explained. I would mention in this regard only that, if a procedural difference, such as concreteness of the materials, were the critical factor, we would expect to see an across-the board difference in performance in the two domains (rather than one that appeared on some indicators and not others). Specifically, a difference postulated both by us and by Klahr and Carver—that theories in the social domain are both cognitively and affectively richer than theories in the physical domain—receives support from our data: The major performance differences that we observed, such as the difficulty in relinquishing causal theories, were ones that this hypothesis would predict.

Among their "Suggestions for Future Studies," Klahr and Carver recommend including a condition in which subjects investigate the database in the absence of any probes of their reasoning. We have contemplated such a condition, and collecting these data most likely warrants a place on our "to do" list. Two points bear mention, however. First, the questions that we put to subjects did more than serve as a scaffold supporting their investigative activity (and hence a form of training). They also served the critical methodological purpose of externalizing subjects' reasoning; without this aid, we would have had little opportunity to observe the reasoning underlying either their investigative strategies or their conclusions. Second, the form of intervention was dictated theoretically by what we regarded as its essential component—the exercise of thinking. The fact has been widely noted that it is not easy to get people to think. Asking questions was our means of implementing exercise of subjects' thinking. Had we instructed subjects simply to go off and find out about each of the problem environments, most likely we would have witnessed a rush of data gathering and not very much thinking (the essential component of the intervention hence lost). The ultimate outcome under this condition is also broadly predictable: less adequate strategy usage and inferior knowledge acquisition. It does not follow that this condition is not worth examining—the magnitude of the difference between the two conditions would tell us a number of things worth knowing. And Klahr and Carver are of course quite right that claiming exercise as a sufficient condition for change does not explain the process. Questions of process are the difficult ones that remain, as noted earlier. Still, the thesis that exercise of thinking is a sufficient condition for its transformation has received little formal empirical documentation, despite the prevalent attention it has been given in the theoretical literature.

I conclude with an issue that has occupied an important place in my thinking for many years—integrating qualitative and quantitative methods of data analysis. I accept Klahr and Carver's judgment that we have not yet gone as far as we might in this respect. The limitations of exclusively quantitative analyses restricted to response frequencies in preconceived categories have by now been well noted: even within the confines of these categories, individual patterns of performance are lost, but more damaging still is the distance to be bridged between these categories and the real thinking of individuals, especially when, as examined in this *Monograph,* people have freedom in directing their own thought. As attested by another recent *Monograph* (Demetriou, Efklides, & Platsidou, 1993) methodologically very different but on a topic related to ours, new, more powerful quantitative methods may enhance the precision and range of inferences that developmentalists can draw, but they do not reduce this distance. At the other extreme, exclusively qualitative data do not allow as powerful inferences as we would like to make.

How, then, does one bridge the gap? As authors, we confronted the additional challenge of presenting our work in a way that would convey the complexity of the phenomena without leaving the reader struggling to find the forest in an unwieldy mass of trees. The tables in Chapters III and IV to which Klahr and Carver refer are in fact a very good case in point, one of quite a few of this sort that we debated in preparing this *Monograph.* How should we trade off the quick picture of overall knowledge acquisition that these tables provide against the additional insight to be gleaned from a more complex set of tables that laid out all the many possible patterns of individual change? Similarly, would the addition of evolving prediction scores add enough to the already complex and detail-laden qualitative portrayals of change to have warranted the added burden on the reader? We do not claim to have gotten this balance exactly right. Nor have we entirely met the objective of linking qualitative and quantitative data as different pictures of what are in the end the same phenomena. In an early version of this *Monograph,* we integrated presentation of qualitative and quantitative data to a greater extent, but that approach turned out to be unwieldy in allowing systematic sequential presentation of a complicated set of results.

If the task is the difficult one of examining the nature of developmental change, the challenge is even greater. Although not the only approach, the best methodological bet at present, I propose, is to center analysis around intensive individual case studies of change (observed microgenetically) that incorporate all the quantitative and qualitative indicators that appear to be informative, with appropriate summary at an aggregate level. A subsequent task is to decide the level of detail at which these findings are best reported.

One of our hopes in publishing this *Monograph* is that it will motivate others to pursue such efforts and to refine the approach we have taken. At the broadest level, detailed examination of qualitative data, direct observation of change, process comparisons across multiple cohorts, a dual focus on knowledge and strategy, and attention to "meta-" components of cognition are all features that I hope to see increasingly become characteristics of developmental research.

## References

Demetriou, A., Efklides, A., & Platsidou, M. (1993). The architecture and dynamics of developing mind: Experiential structuralism as a frame for unifying cognitive developmental theories. *Monographs of the Society for Research in Child Development,* **58** (5–6, Serial No. 234).

Holland, J., Holyoak, K., Nisbett, R., & Thagard, P. (1986). *Induction: Processes of inference, learning, and discovery.* Cambridge, MA: MIT Press.

# CONTRIBUTORS

**Deanna Kuhn** (Ph.D. 1969, University of California, Berkeley) is a professor of psychology and education at Teachers College, Columbia University. Her research focuses on the development and use of formal and informal reasoning in children, adolescents, and adults.

**Merce Garcia-Mila** (Ph.D. 1992, Columbia University) is a postdoctoral research associate at the University of Barcelona (Spain). Her research interests include the development of scientific reasoning, preadolescents' mathematical understanding, and their application to science learning.

**Anat Zohar** (Ph.D. 1991, Hebrew University of Jerusalem) is an assistant professor in the Department of Science Education at the Technion, Haifa, Israel. She has been a postdoctoral research associate at Teachers College, Columbia University, under fellowships from the Lady Davis Fellowship Trust and the James S. McDonnell Foundation and later worked at the Hebrew University of Jerusalem under a fellowship from the Wolf Foundation. Her main interest is the development of higher-order thinking skills within the science curriculum.

**Christopher Andersen** (M.A. 1990, Columbia University) is a Ph.D. candidate at Teachers College, Columbia University. His research interests include children's scientific reasoning and the role of peer collaboration in its development.

**Sheldon H. White** (Ph.D. 1957, University of Iowa) has taught at the University of Chicago and Harvard University. He has done research on children's learning and cognitive development, has worked on social programs and policies for children, and has written about the history of developmental psychology. He is currently the John Lindsley Professor of Psychology at Harvard.

**David Klahr** (Ph.D. 1968, Carnegie Mellon University) is professor of psychology and director of the Literacy in Science Center at Carnegie Mellon University. He is the author of *Cognitive Development: An Information Processing View* (with J. G. Wallace, 1976) and the editor of *Cognition and Instruction* (1976), *Production System Models of Learning and Development* (with P. Langley and R. Neches, 1987), and *Complex Information Processing: The Impact of Herbert A. Simon* (with K. Kotovsky, 1989). His recent research on the development of problem-solving and scientific-reasoning skills is reported in *Cognitive Psychology* and *Child Development*.

**Sharon M. Carver** (Ph.D. 1986, Carnegie Mellon University) is the director of the Children's School (Carnegie Mellon's laboratory preschool and kindergarten) and an adjunct associate professor of psychology at Carnegie Mellon University. Her research interests include the development of problem-solving skills, the application of cognitive models of specific skills to the design of instruction and assessment at all age levels, and the uses of computer and video technology to facilitate both research and teaching.

## STATEMENT OF EDITORIAL POLICY

The *Monographs* series is intended as an outlet for major reports of developmental research that generate authoritative new findings and use these to foster a fresh and/or better-integrated perspective on some conceptually significant issue or controversy. Submissions from programmatic research projects are particularly welcome; these may consist of individually or group-authored reports of findings from some single large-scale investigation or of a sequence of experiments centering on some particular question. Multiauthored sets of independent studies that center on the same underlying question can also be appropriate; a critical requirement in such instances is that the various authors address common issues and that the contribution arising from the set as a whole be both unique and substantial. In essence, irrespective of how it may be framed, any work that contributes significant data and/or extends developmental thinking will be taken under editorial consideration.

Submissions should contain a minimum of 80 manuscript pages (including tables and references); the upper limit of 150–175 pages is much more flexible (please submit four copies; a copy of every submission and associated correspondence is deposited eventually in the archives of the SRCD). Neither membership in the Society for Research in Child Development nor affiliation with the academic discipline of psychology are relevant; the significance of the work in extending developmental theory and in contributing new empirical information is by far the most crucial consideration. Because the aim of the series is not only to advance knowledge on specialized topics but also to enhance cross-fertilization among disciplines or subfields, it is important that the links between the specific issues under study and larger questions relating to developmental processes emerge as clearly to the general reader as to specialists on the given topic.

Potential authors who may be unsure whether the manuscript they are planning would make an appropriate submission are invited to draft an outline of what they propose and send it to the Editor for assessment. This mechanism, as well as a more detailed description of all editorial policies, evaluation processes, and format requirements, is given in the "Guidelines for the Preparation of *Monographs* Submissions," which can be obtained by writing to the Editor, Rachel K. Clifton, Department of Psychology, University of Massachusetts, Amherst, MA 01003.